HAPPY HIKER

The Epic Journey of an Unlikely
Appalachian Trail Thru-Hiker

MAX MASON

Published in Australia by
Helgo Media
Email: Max@mmhmason.com
Website: www.maxmasonauthor.com

First published in Australia 2020
Copyright © Max Mason 2020

All rights reserved. No part of this publication may be reproduced, stored in a retrieval system, or transmitted, in any form or by any means without the prior written permission of the publisher, nor be otherwise circulated in any form of binding or cover other than that in which it is published and without a similar condition being imposed on the subsequent purchaser.

National Library of Australia Cataloguing in Publication entry

 A catalogue record for this book is available from the National Library of Australia

ISBN: 978-0-6450586-0-4 (paperback)
ISBN: 978-0-6450586-1-1 (hardback)
ISBN: 978-0-6450586-3-5 (epub)

Printed by Ingram Spark

Cover photography by Max Mason
Design by Sophie White

All care has been taken in the preparation of the information herein, but no responsibility can be accepted by the publisher or author for any damages resulting from the misinterpretation of this work. All contact details given in this book were current at the time of publication, but are subject to change.

The advice given in this book is based on the experience of the individuals. Professionals should be consulted for individual problems. The author and publisher shall not be responsible for any person with regard to any loss or damage caused directly or indirectly by the information in this book.

*This book is dedicated to Helen and Mungo
who are my why.*

*My sincere gratitude goes to my editor,
Peter E. C. Dashwood who knew when to time and
balance tough love and encouragement perfectly.*

*I pay tribute to and recognize with immense respect:
The Appalachian Trail Conservancy (ATC),
the Appalachian Mountain Clubs, and all the
volunteers and trail maintainers who protect
The Trail and make hiking a safe and
enjoyable experience.*

PRAISE FOR *HAPPY HIKER*

"Max recounts precisely what it's like to endure a 2000+ mile walk along the physical and mental rollercoaster known as the Appalachian Trail. He captured the highs, lows, trials, tribulations and characters he met along the way in poetic form. I thru-hiked the trail all over again."

Joe Fubel – GA-ME Class of '01

"Happy's glorious epic poem perfectly captures the trail experience in all its beautiful, wild, wonderful and sometimes challenging moments. His tips for a successful thru-hike are spot on."

TwoBadDogs – Triple Crown Thru-hikers

"Max offers solid advice for anyone considering a long-distance trail. The epic poem of Happy's hike is entertaining and full of AT thru-hiker wisdom, do's and don'ts, as well as lessons learned the hard way for his next adventure."

John Wilson – 3X AT Thru-hiker

"Max Mason has re-invented the epic adventure poem for everyday people which magically draws you in as if you are experiencing the highs and lows of the Trail with him. Easy to read, engaging, funny and relatable to us all I hope this becomes a popular new genre."

Mark Stewart – Hiker

"HH is an epic poem describing Max's transformation from Joe Average to long distance hiker, tackling the challenges of everyday miles to be covered while overcoming loneliness and absence from family and friends. A must read for anyone wanting to walk off the beaten track over multiple days."

Graeme Horsley – 3x Camino pilgrim walker

"Max has described his experience of the trail using poems that help keep your attention and wanting more. He explains the trials and errors endured during a thru-hike. A very relatable and easy read for those with a dream of a thru-hike or those who just like to read about adventures."

> Bev Whitehead – A hiker that believes it's all about the journey

"Max Mason shows that you can do anything you put your mind too, you don't need to be a hiker to enjoy this story, and a refreshing poem format that just keeps you wanting more."

> Lisa Tringali – Hiker, Photographer, Nature Enthusiast

"It brought back a lot of memories of my time on the trail. I felt like I was on the trail again."

> Philip Anderson – Thru-hiker, Retired

"Max Mason undersells himself in this book. He is a remarkable man and I felt as if I was on the trail with him. I loved how he was so open with his feelings, raw and tough, digging deep. Quietly ecstatic when he reached Katahdin's peck. A must read for anyone looking for an adventure."

> Karen Holmes – Adventure marathon/multi-sport athlete

"In this epic poem of the Appalachian trail, Max Mason chronicles his thru-hike of the famous pathway. Along the way he shares his secrets to successfully mastering the mental challenges that inevitably accompany the 2100 mile journey. At times funny, at times serious, but always engaging, this poem should be on everyone's list of guidebooks for planning their thru-hike."

> Brad Whitcomb – AT Thru-hiker 2015

CONTENTS

	Introduction	9
1	25 Steps to Successfully Thru-hiking the Appalachian Trail	15
2	Trail Terminology (& Other Useful Facts)	27
3	Map of the Appalachian Trail	37
4	The Cast of Characters	41
5	The Happy Hiker Epic Poem	45
6	Epilogue	242
7	An Infinite Moment on Pleasant River	247
	Glossary	249
	About the Author	257

INTRODUCTION

This book was written by someone who had no business completing one of the most grueling ultra-distance hikes on the planet – the Appalachian Trail. I hope to entertain readers with an adventure story which shows that ordinary people can do extraordinary things if they acquire the right skills and attitudes.

For most of my life I had never shown any great stamina or capacity for endurance. At high school I didn't excel in any of the major sports. I was in the bottom half in cross-country, and mediocre at athletics. I liked reading and spending time alone in nature.

Workwise I didn't stick to any one career and any successes I've had have been due to good interpersonal skills rather than sticking to one thing. I tried to write a novel once and it sits half finished. My bookcase and Kindle reader is littered with half-finished books. I'm a great starter, but not much of a finisher.

In many ways I was Joe Average.

So, given my personality, how did I complete the Appalachian Trail when it's all about grit, willpower, resilience, stamina and the ability to endure – or so we assume? Qualities I didn't appear to possess.

My secret is that I have an insatiable curiosity about what makes people tick, and that has made all the difference.

The first time I used psychology on myself was when I successfully gave up smoking in my mid-20's. I had tried and failed several times, then came up with the idea of psyching myself out of smoking. I wrote a list of all the reasons why I needed to give up, duplicated it, and stuck them on walls all around my apartment. For two months every time I saw a list, I read it three times. In that way I drummed into myself why I should give up. On my 26th birthday I threw away my cigarettes and haven't had one for thirty years.

Finding your 'why' is the secret to success in nearly everything. I believe with absolute certainty that every one of us has the ability to create positive change in our lives by reframing our perceptions and our reality. One of the best ways to do this is by identifying our why. Understanding "why" you are doing something is the bedrock of motivation, and motivation is the essential ingredient for handling difficult tasks.

When I became interested in thru-hiking the Appalachian Trail (AT) I initially focused on researching on-line gear options, as most people do. Then luckily, I came across a book called Appalachian Trials by Zach Davis. Zach correctly identified that the key to thru-hiking the AT is mostly in the head. Amongst many other excellent recommendations is writing three lists before you start:

- 'I am thru-hiking the Appalachian Trail because… (this is your 'why')

- When I successfully thru-hike the Appalachian Trail, I will… (these are the personal benefits you'll acquire upon reaching Katahdin)

- If I give up on the Appalachian Trail, I will… (these are the negative perceptions you'll develop of yourself if you quit – harsh but effective).' (Appalachian Trials by Zach Davis, 2012)

Of course, when I saw the three lists, I strongly identified with the process, and diligently wrote mine out. I am grateful to Zach for probably being the difference between me thru-hiking and giving up.

OK, so why did I write an epic poem entitled, '*Happy Hiker: The Epic Journey of an Unlikely Appalachian Trail Thru-hiker?*'

When I returned to my home in New Zealand after the AT, I gave the usual slide presentation talks to groups such as Rotary and hiking groups. These became very popular and I gave over 50 talks. The basis for their popularity was that I didn't merely show lots of scenic photos of mountains, tell amusing stories and imply how tough I was. Instead, I focused on how somebody without a history of physical endurance could succeed, when about 75% of people who attempt the AT, fail. I told them about the inner game of thru-hiking which motivates you to walk a half marathon a day, six days a week, for six months. That's about 150 half marathons.

I told them of the mental techniques I used to keep going when I was exhausted and every muscle in my body was screaming at me to stop. I also broadened my presentational message to show that these mental techniques can be applied to any part of life when the going is tough. Ultimately, that's my message to you. If an ordinary person like me can succeed in a thru-hike then all of us are capable of far more than we ever imagine.

Why an epic poem? What I particularly like about poetry is that it can be very succinct. Poetry has the capability to condense thoughts and imply stuff that takes more words to write as prose. The metre and flow of a poem seemed appropriate to the onward march of the Trail.

Epic poetry is supposed to follow a number of conventions, and in particular the protagonist must be a hero. Conversely, my epic poem is about an anti-hero: me.

Another motivation for this work stems from my love of adventure books and movies and I am fascinated by the idea behind Joseph Campbell's 'The Hero's Journey', or monomyth. The concept behind the monomyth is that all cultures share the common template of a story where the hero sets off on an adventure, survives or wins in a decisive crisis and returns home transformed or with new knowledge. That certainly happened to me.

If you don't know much about the AT, I suggest you read Chapter Three on AT terminology, and remember there is a glossary too. You could also familiarize yourself with it through the Appalachian Trail Conservatory, ALDHA (Appalachian Long Distance Hikers association), Wikipedia, or one of the myriad of websites or books written on the subject. YouTube is also a good resource.

Here's a quick background about myself to provide some context:

I was born in Rhodesia (now Zimbabwe), and lived most of my early years in a small mining village in the remote African bush. My Dad worked on the mine, and my Mom was a bank manager. I have two wonderful younger sisters.

I studied psychology at university, worked for a few years, travelled the world, spent some time in California, and went on to start a couple of small businesses. After Helen and I were married in 1990 we left Zimbabwe for the UK, studied for Masters degrees, and then worked in Scotland for six years. After our son Mungo was born, we immigrated to New Zealand where we have been very happy. I had a succession of management and business advisory roles before embarking on my AT adventure.

In 2014 Helen was awarded a Harkness Fellowship to undertake health research in the USA for 12 months with the Institute for Healthcare Improvement. I gained a visa for six months, stopped off at Boston where Helen was staying and hit the Trail, hiking northbound from Springer Mountain on 20 March 2015. Helen joined me on the Trail several times.

I summited Mount Katahdin 178 days later on 13 September just two days before my visa expired and then rushed to Boston to catch my return flight to New Zealand.

After the hike when I returned to New Zealand, I was persuaded to stand in the elections for the mayoralty in our city of Tauranga, in the Bay of Plenty. Prior to my success on the AT, I would never have had the confidence to do so. I didn't become mayor, but was elected as a city councilor for a term of three years. I also successfully ran two marathons with my newfound mental strength. Last year I cycled across Australia (unsupported) from Adelaide to Darwin which is 3000km (1888 miles), through the desert. This is the equivalent distance of New Orleans to Los Angeles. The AT trail changed me profoundly and gave me the confidence and ability to do these things.

I caught COVID in March 2020, and when I can get rid of the long-term effects of intermittent fatigue, I intend to kayak Australia's longest River, the Murray, from source to sea which is 2,508 km (1,558 mi).

Thru-hiking the AT has given me an unshakable belief that we can all overcome our self-limiting beliefs and achieve more than we would have dreamed. Starting a business, going for that big job, writing a book – it's all within our grasp.

MAX MASON

1

25 STEPS TO SUCCESSFULLY THRU-HIKING THE APPALACHIAN TRAIL

Based on my AT experience I have developed a list of 25 steps on how anyone can thru-hike the AT.

The first ten should be done well before the hike is started.

The next ten relate to on the Trail, and the last five, on making the most of the success afterwards.

The principles behind these steps can be applied to any huge task that you may be required, or simply wish, to undertake in the future.

Remember – the Appalachian Trail takes about 5,000,000 steps to complete. If you decide to thru-hike and follow these first 25 steps you are far more likely to be in the 25% of hikers who succeed!

It is important to note that these 25 steps worked for me, and many of the successful hikers I know. Invariably however, others will have a different view and a different journey. Many paths can lead to the same destination.

Before you start (10 steps)

1. Find your REASON for doing it (why). Do you really, really love something about the Trail or hiking? Clarify what it is. For example, I love seeing the detail of nature unfolding in Spring through Summer, into Autumn. I find it endlessly fascinating. Hiking the AT allowed me to do that for six months. Seeing nature change through the seasons was a transcendent experience for me. So, find your why. An excellent way is to buy Zach Davis' book, "Appalachian Trials" and follow his advice on lists which I have covered above.

2. Go public. As soon as you tell your family and friends you put pressure on yourself. Pressure is good as long it is translated into determination to succeed, not into unhelpful stress.

3. Visualize success (as defined by you). I thought continually about how I would communicate the Trail experience to audiences, and I knew I couldn't do that if I failed to complete it. Others just think about that sign on the summit of Katahdin.

4. Solve the niggling questions about possible difficulties before you go.

    - The best thing to do is speak to someone who has thru-hiked, preferably about your age.

    - I worried about how hard a 3,000 feet mountain was going to be. I found a 1000m mountain in NZ and hiked it. No problem! It built my confidence.

- I worried that I wouldn't be able to hike 20-mile days, which I would need to. So, I did a couple on the weekends, and it wasn't that bad.

- I worried about getting mentally bored if I was hiking for 8-10 hours a day six days a week. So, I experimented with podcasts, and audio books, training courses and music, and found after a morning of hiking while observing nature, I lost concentration and started listening to books on headphones. I loved learning new things while I hiked.

5. Do the physical training. It will give you emotional confidence as well. On the Trail you will be on your feet with a heavy pack over eight hours a day. You'll never get totally trail fit beforehand but try to hike at least two hours per weekday, and four hours per weekend day, for the month before you start. Include as many hills as possible. If you can't spare those hours, then get running fit (especially hill training), and try and lose weight.

6. Simulate as much of the Trail as possible. This will minimize surprises and unexpected discomfort in the first few weeks on the Trail:

   a. Physical and mental – Follow the great Warren Doyle's advice that the best predictor of AT success is to hike the 272-mile Long Trail in Vermont in 21-25 days. Warren has hiked the AT 18 times and assists people to thru-hike in expeditions. If it's not possible for you do the Long Trail, then hike, and sleep in your tent, as much as time allows. Yes, we've all had our family and neighbors laugh at us when we pitch our new tents and sleep several nights in the back garden! Especially when you are 55!

    b. Get to know your equipment, especially your boots and what it's like having a 30lb pack on your back for hours at a time.

7. Test out your equipment. Don't get hung up on online research for hiking equipment. Yes, it's great fun, but it's better to spend time breaking in your boots and getting fit than obsessing about which ultralight socks are the best

8. Be prepared to change. Be aware that if you are an emotionally and/or physically sensitive person who is often critical or are easily upset about things, like the exact temperature of your food, or not getting bitten by bugs, then the AT may not be for you. Or, you will need to undergo some personal transformation. Successful thru-hikers don't sweat the small stuff – the heat, cold, wet, chaffing, insect bites, injuries, uncertainty, hunger, thirst, mistakes, misunderstandings, getting lost, weird people etc. There is a constant level of discomfort for 4-6 months. If you have the capacity to tolerate and accept it you'll be fine, but if you haven't, you must develop it.

9. Learn about emotional intelligence. Understand the importance of your emotions on the hike. You will feel an emotional intensity not normally found in your normal life. Your emotions can be your friend or your enemy. Having the ability to step outside yourself, recognize and analyze what you are feeling, and why is critical. Knowing when you are feeling despondent for example allows you to intervene and use self-motivational techniques to change how you feel. Don't let negativity fester and grow.

To keep yourself pushing on when you are physically and mentally tired will take determination and strength of will. This is emotional energy and intensity and it's a skill to raise it up and maintain it for long periods. I guess I'm a bit old school when it comes to displaying emotions. I normally only cry for family bereavements, but I found on the Trail, I cried several times. The intensity brings emotions to the surface.

a. Self-awareness. Seek to understand your emotions and develop the skill of observing them and influencing them, through self-control techniques (self-talk, meditation, breathing, changing your mood though music, stories etc.).

b. Empathy for the emotions of others. This is also important as emotions are very low and very high sometimes. It's uplifting to be able to encourage and motivate others who are going through a hard time. If you hike as part of a team you can support each other.

Ultimately, it's about controlling your negative emotions and having a proactive, positive attitude. If you can do that, you will succeed.

10. Anticipate a large number of setbacks. Every day things will not go the way you planned. Your job is to be a problem solver. Remember you are going to be way out of your comfort zone, which is why so many people give up so early. As time goes on, daily hiking becomes your comfort zone. But you will still get injuries and things happening. Roll with them.

During your hike (10 steps)

11. Cultivate an attitude of acceptance. If it's raining, it's raining. Don't hate it or be annoyed or have some other emotional reaction. Just accept it and adapt. If it's very cold you may need wet weather gear, but in the warm months it's often better to just hike through the rain in a tee-shirt and dry out later. It's a good mental trick to be able to distinguish between the controllable and uncontrollable.

    Closely related to acceptance of what you can't control is faith. There's a brilliant aphorism, 'The Trail will provide,' which is so true. So often, you'll be given some Trail Magic food when you really need it or get a ride into town just before the post office closes. If you believe good things will happen, they are far more likely to.

12. Be grateful for what you are experiencing. The AT is probably a unique one-off life experience. Taking lots of photos and writing a diary (even if it's just a few notes), reinforces how fortunate you are. Think of the millions of people in cubicle farms who envy you.

13. Monitor your emotions and develop a tool-box of motivational statements. Practice self-awareness and use the tools to control your self-limiting emotions and beliefs. To overcome my limiting beliefs, self-doubts, and mental exhaustion I invented two acronyms NIV and PIV (Negative Inner Voice (NIV) and Positive Inner Voice (PIV).

    As the Trail progressed, I developed a toolbox of self-talk techniques. When I felt lousy climbing the tenth mountain in the third day of rain, and wanted to stop, I would control NIV by getting PIV to repeat some of the motivational statements below. In that way I would reframe the experience and be more positive.

a. "You don't conquer the mountain you conquer yourself." (Sir Edmund Hillary).

b. This is tough but I'm tougher. I can do this (Mungo Mason).

c. I can't let my supporters down.

d. Others have done this before.

e. Much less able people have done this successfully (shame yourself as young kids and a range of disabled hikers have all thru-hiked the AT).

f. This too shall pass.

g. You can never go up a mountain too slowly (I would put myself into tractor gear, walk very slowly, and use less energy). Deliberately slowing down was incredibly important to my success.

h. There is always a way. There is always a solution.

i. One day at a time. It's a great mind set to just think about getting through today.

Your Trail name is important. I deliberately choose "Happy" beforehand as I knew sometimes I wouldn't be happy, but if people called me that, it would subtly reinforce my happy perspective. Ensure you get one that sustains and elevates you.

Be aware of the impact of timing on your emotions. I got emotionally down when I was hungry or at the end of the day. It's great to have that "Aha!" breakthrough thought, when you realize that a quick rest and a Snickers Bar will lift your spirits. Men and women differ but as a general rule of thumb but you may need to double the number of calories you eat on the Trail. Think about the balance between carbs and protein. I struggled to get that right for several weeks and dropped weight dramatically. I settled two Ramen noodles and a packet of tuna for dinner, and protein powder with muesli breakfast. Then a bagel and heaps of nuts and energy bars during the day. Everybody's dietary needs and metabolism are different. This worked for me; find what works for you.

14. Be determined to succeed but know your limits. It takes force of will to push yourself to keep hiking when you're tired and someone is offering you a ride to a warm, dry hostel near a craft brewery. It takes bloody-mindedness to keep going and its emotionally intense. It is easy to become distracted and the more you delay and go off trail, the slower you go, and your sense of determination is undermined. Maintain that strength of will. A great way to stick to your average miles per day, is to think of your time on the trail as a job, or occupation. It's not a weekend hike or camping trip, it's what you do.

There is a balance here of course, you can't be too obsessive. You do have to stop and smell the roses, and enjoy yourself, but be aware of how easy it is to lose your momentum.

A common characteristic of many hikers was that many are driven to hike too fast too soon and either cause an injury, or they lose the enjoyment of it. Natural competitiveness can be the cause or an inability to know their bodies and push past the physical limits everyone has. Please go slowly for the first few weeks, then increase your daily milage.

Some people are prone to making impulsive decisions. They say you should never decide to leave the Trail on a bad day.

That's very true. Sometimes hikers would have knee or other problems and after a few days give up without persevering.

15. Find your mental refuge. Practice mindfulness and live in the present moment as much as possible. You may find you develop a daily routine. Mine was to look at the passing of the forest for the morning. Then after lunch I'd start listening to educational audio courses e.g. 101 university courses. The last few hours when I was physically and mentally very tired I would listen to fiction such as Game of Thrones, which would transport me into a different place, and I would feel less pain.

16. Share your burdens. It's very comforting to be hiking with your buddies and have a good old grouse, or a laugh when the day is over. A burden shared is a burden halved. However, it's important to be with people you click with. It grates when you feel you are stuck with people you don't identify with.

17. Hike your own hike. You have to make many decisions that may been seen as selfish by others. Nothing should get in the way of summitting Katahdin. You may make small compromises that may cause a delay, like a few hours or a day for a new trail buddy with a rolled ankle. Anything more, is a serious delay to your success. Be prepared to be centered on your own success, and also that others will have the same mindset. Don't be offended if someone doesn't want to hike with you because you are too slow or procrastinate. Those are the rules.

18. Keep the end goal in mind. Say "no" to every distraction. Some groups have a lot of fun in the trail towns, and their groups get slower and slower, and people start dropping out. Keep your absolute commitment to your purpose and maintain your momentum. I was lucky because I had a six-month visa period

before I had to depart the USA and that commitment pushed me along. Having a deadline can be helpful. Be aware your average hiking miles per day will decrease substantially in New Hampshire and Maine (mine halved).

19. Don't sweat the small stuff. Understand the difference between the small things (the heat, cold, wet, chaffing, insect bites, injuries, uncertainty, hunger, thirst, mistakes, misunderstandings, getting lost etc.), and the important things (serious or long-lasting injuries, problems at home etc.) One of the things that might seem small but can grow are foot problems such as blisters. Stop immediately and sort them out, or they may grow into big issues. Big hint – carry leukotape for blisters.

20. Emotional support from off-trail. Helen and Mungo gave me unequivocal support. They visited me on the trail, sent food parcels and got friends and family to post encouraging FaceBook messages when I was having a hard time. Also, they held their tongues when I was being a dick when I was emotionally intense. Conversely, I saw trail buddies who were having trouble at home, or didn't get the support they needed, and it really dragged them down. It's really important to resolve any potential domestic issues before you start.

After the hike (5 steps)

Success is much more than physically completing the Trail. Many people are forever changed by the experience. The five steps below give some ideas of how you may be changed. Be aware however that it won't happen immediately. After the euphoria it will take a year or two to assimilate how the Trail may have changed you.

21. You've learned some skills. For me the most important was: 'how to keep going when the going gets tough'. It might be something different for you. These skills may benefit other aspects of your life.

22. You've learned some truths about yourself or others. For me it was that we all have far more potential than we dare to imagine. Post AT I ran two marathons, was elected as a City Councilor and cycled across Australia in the desert.

23. You will achieve some personal transformation. You will probably become far more internally confident and self-assured. Hopefully a bit humbler too, because only you and just a few others know how incredibly hard it was. At every BBQ or social gathering whenever the topic of hiking or the outdoors comes up some friend will tell everyone that you thru-hiked the AT. It's actually quite cool.

24. You might develop a framework for living. In the years afterwards I developed an interest in the philosophy of Stoicism, which I was practicing without knowing it on the Trail. There are hundreds of free hours to learn from audio books and educational courses. On the other hand, there's a thru-hiker's tee-shirt slogan: 'The AT will ruin your life.' Let's just say there have been many career changes after the Trail!

25. You will be more self-aware. You will unquestionably know more about yourself and your ability to adapt to difficulty. Important for me was the realization of how little we need to survive. It's incredibly liberating to know that all the material stuff we have around is nice to have, but not really necessary.

I strongly believe that if you follow the 25 steps you can successfully thru-hike the Appalachian or any other long-distance trail. If you have read between the lines you will see they are a resilience blueprint for the other times in life when the going gets tough.

A note about the verses. Each day is covered by a 12-line poem and a photograph. Some days there was so much going on, I couldn't fit it into 12-lines so it might spill over into the next day.

A note about each day's title. The title of each day pertains to the day, the place where I spent the night, the State, and the distance hiked that day, for example: Day 68. Bryant Ridge Shelter. VA. 20.8m

2

TRAIL TERMINOLOGY (& OTHER USEFUL FACTS)

Advil. A painkiller also branded as Ibuprofen which is known as 'Vitamin I,' as so many thru-hikers consume it.

AMC. Appalachian Mountain Club.

Appalachian Trail Conservancy (ATC). The non-profit organization dedicated to the conservation of the AT and was founded in 1925. It is responsible for the daily management of the AT in agreement with the National Park Service. It coordinates thirty-one Appalachian Trail maintaining clubs who do the on-the-ground maintenance work. Most trail work is performed by 6,000 volunteers.

AT Guide by AWOL Miller. This may be the most popular guidebook, and the one I used. The Appalachian Conservancy also publishes one, and various apps are also popular. They provide a wealth of information such as distance between shelters and other features, all water sources, elevation, maps of towns along the way, contact details for hostels and shuttle drivers, and a myriad of other useful information.

Audie Murphy. Murphy was one of the most decorated soldiers in WW2. 'To Hell and Back' was a movie he starred in, playing himself, when he returned from the war.

Balds. Refers to the grassy tops of otherwise thickly wooded hills, especially in the Southern Appalachians. It is a mystery why some balds exist, where similar nearby hills are completely covered with forest. Balds allow hikers to experience rare views.

Bear video. I took a video of a mother bear and cubs incident: *https://www.nzherald.co.nz/bay-of-plenty-times/video/black-bear-spotted-on-the-appalachian-trail/Y2ZV3V75JYWJL4DUCZY76W666M/*

Benton MacKaye. Envisioned the AT in 1921 on Stratton Mountain. He was the dreamer.

Bill Bryson. Bryson wrote a best-selling book 'A Walk in the Woods: Rediscovering America on the Appalachian Trail,' in 1998. Many thru-hikers resent the fact he made money from the book but only hiked 870 miles. His hiking companion in the book was Steven Katz, who some say did not exist, but it is well documented that he did.

Bubble. This is the hiking group that roughly moves at the same speed over long distances. You may not see some people for a few days then they reappear.

Darn Tough. A well-known brand of hiking sock.

Dartmouth College. Is one of eight Ivy League universities, and is located in Hanover, New Hampshire.

Goose, Spice and Cap. These three young environmentalists were sponsored by Granite Gear and successfully packed out 1,090 pounds of trail trash. They would empty their bags at nearby towns recording the weight disposed of.

Earl Schaffer. The first person to thru-hike the AT. He saw action in the Pacific in WW2 and said he hiked the whole distance of the AT in 1948 to "walk off the war".

Flipflop hike. A few thru-hikers flip flop hike which refers to the practice of hiking a mix of non-sequential sections of the Trail, but who complete the full distance in one calendar year. Warm-and-Toasty for example had two cars, and would drive one north, park it at the trailhead, and hike south to the second car. She would drive that to a trailhead about a day's hike beyond the first car, and repeat the process.

Fugitive Movie. Fontana Dam is often mistakenly identified as the location for the 1993 Harrison Ford movie 'Fugitive'. In fact it was nearby Cheoah Dam. Ford plays Dr Kimble who is arrested for a murder he did not commit, escapes and is on the run from the police for most of the movie.

Grandma Gatewood. The first woman to thru-hike the AT, in 1955, at the age of 67. She also was the first person to hike it three times. The last time was in 1963 at 75 years old.

Green Tunnel. A nickname for the AT as so much of it is spent hiking through thick woods and rhododendron tunnels. One can spend days hiking witout a decent view.

Guillotine. A rock passage with a suspended rock above hikers who have to squeeze through.

Harpers Ferry, WV. The psychological mid-point of the Trail. The Appalachian Trail Conservancy (ATC) which administers the AT is located there. Harpers Ferry is of great historical importance to the Civil War era. It changed hands eight times in the Civil War and was heavily damaged (Harpers Ferry not the ATC!).

Hike your own hike. A common saying on the AT. It means you have permission to make decisions for your own benefit without fear of criticism. For example, leaving behind a slower friend if they are nursing an injury.

Ice Cream Challenge. Is a Trail tradition. The intention is to eat a quart (1 litre) of ice cream as quickly as possible.

Jennifer Pharr Davis. A long-distance hiker who held the Fastest Known Time for the AT (for male and female), until this was beaten by Scott Jurek in 2015. She is also an author, speaker, National Geographic Adventurer of the Year, and Ambassador for the American Hiking Society.

Keffer Oak. The largest oak tree on the AT in the southern states is about 300 years old.

Lehigh Gap. For almost a century a zinc factory polluted Lehigh Gap with chemicals that killed vegetation and other life. Its environmental restoration was funded by Superfund.

Lyme Disease. Deer ticks carry and transmitt this debilitating disease. If not treated it can cause a range of long-lasting heath issues. One survey found 9% of hikers contracted Lyme disease. A telltale 'bullseye' rash indicates one may have Lyme. Some hikers get treated and can return to hiking. DEET is a popular insect repellent to control deer ticks. Inspecting ones' skin for ticks daily is wise.

Mount Washington. The highest peak in the Northeastern United States at 6,288 ft. Changeable weather and poor planning have created its reputation for a dangerous hike. Nearly 150 people have died on the mountain since 1849.

Moxie. A carbonated drink invented by a Mainer in the 1800's. It was marketed as a health drink and features Gentian as an ingredient.

Murder on the AT. Since 1974 there have been 11 murders on the Appalachian Trail. Meredith Hope Emerson (24) was murdered near Blood Mountain in 2008.

Myron Avery. The practical doer who was most responsible for driving the completion of the AT. He was a long-time chairman of the Appalachian Trail Conference, and he both clashed and collaborated with Benton MacKaye, and others. Avery Peak is named after him.

Nalgene. A popular water bottle brand.

Neel Gap. The first real stop for north bound thru-hikers. It has an outfitter shop and a tree with hundreds of old boots hanging from it.

Nero. Means nearly zero – just a short hike.

Newspaper articles on my hike:
https://www.nzherald.co.nz/bay-of-plenty-times/news/trailblazer-nears-end-of-epic-hike/Y2FMDQEEQUUV3P2MZD3FLMVAPM/

https://www.nzherald.co.nz/bay-of-plenty-times/news/on-the-record-max-mason/RSGLEXWNKHTF77FGJUY3IDQHZM/

New York-North Jersey Chapter. The second largest of the 12 regional chapters of the Appalachian Mountain Club (AMC).

NOBO. Most thru-hikers start at the south terminus of the Trail and hike north in one sequence. They are called Northbounders or NOBOs.

Outfitters. These are physical and online outdoors recreation retailers.

Purists (or white blazers) are those hikers who insist on hiking every inch of the Trail, with a full pack. They will walk past every single AT white blaze. For example, blue blazes are used to mark other trails leading to shelters, views etc. Most shelters have two paths leading to and from the AT. Typically, these blue blazed trails leading to a shelter, exit the white blazed trail at an angle in the direction of the shelter. Then there is a corresponding blue blazed trail from the shelter to the Trail, joining it further up from where the exit point was. Purists like Walnut, in the morning always walked back to the point they left the Trail the previous evening and resumed their hike from there. Many purists, with the exception of Walnut, had an air of determined superiority about them. A vocabulary has arisen around the color of blazes:

- **Yellow blazing** – skipping portions of the Trail by hitchhiking ahead or getting a ride. This is severely frowned on by most hikers.

- **Aqua blazing** – missing portions of the trail by traveling by canoe or kayak. Because there is white blaze in the Kennebec river canoe, and it's compulsory, it's not considered aqua blazing.

- **Green blazing** – smoking pot on the AT which many young people did.

- **Brown blazing** – refers to hiking with an upset stomach, with frequent need to visit the bush.

- **Pink blazing** – seeking sex or romance on the Trail.

- **Bar blazing** – frequenting trail towns pubs as much as possible.

Rats in Shelters. Shelter rats thrive when hikers don't secure all their food and packaging in sealed food bags hung from bear cables outside. Rats are attracted to discarded food wrappers at night. A rat ate through a plastic zip on my pack to get at a Snickers bar I had forgotten in the hip belt pocket. Black rat snakes are attracted by the rats, and are fairly common around shelters. They are harmless, to humans.

REI – Recreational Equipment, Inc., is a very popular American retail and outdoor recreation chain of stores.

Roller Coaster. A 12.5 mile section with 3500 vertical feet of steep up and down hills, mostly 300-400 foot ascents and descents.

Sam I Am. Sam was a recently resigned career prison warden who thru-hiked to walk off the negativity of prisons. He video interviewed hundreds of hikers (see Youtube). He also wrote an excellent book, 'Sole Searching on the Appalachian Trail.'

Scott Jurek. A ultra-distance runner who beat Jennifer Pharr-Davis' Fastest Known Time by 3h13m to set a new record of 46d 8h 7m. He received a fine from Baxter State Park rangers for, amongst other things, littering when celebratory champagne touched the ground. The controversy raged up and down the Trail for months.

Shake down. This occurs when an experienced hiker goes through everything in a novice hiker's pack and advises what to retain or discard. It's invaluable!

Shelters. Three-sided wooden buildings for hikers to sleep in spaced 6-10 miles apart. Typically allowing 8-12 hikers to sleep like sardines on a platform. They are sited near water sources (mostly streams) and have a decomposition toilet. No running water or electricity. Many hikers sleep in their tents near the shelter and share the communally used outdoor picnic table and bear cables.

Shelter Journal. Every shelter has a shelter journal. Hikers write their names and times of arrival and departure plus notes on weather conditions or to friends. Their function is safety related as they record where the last place of a missing hiker may be. Shelter journals can be very entertaining.

Skyline Drive. The road that runs through or near the Shenandoah National Park. It was built during the Great Depression to create jobs at about the same time as the AT.

Slack-packing. This is the practice of hiking with an almost empty pack. All the heavy items are transported by other means to the next shelter. It's frowned on by purists who believe you should carry your full pack all the way.

SOBO. About 20% of hikers start at Mt Katahdin and hike south and are known as SOBOs.

Stealth camping. Refers to sleeping in a non-designated or illegal area.

Superfund. Provides the Environmental Protection Agency (EPA) funding to restore degraded sites. For almost a century a zinc factory polluted Lehigh Gap with chemicals that killed vegetation and other life. Its environmental restoration was funded by Superfund.

The Presidential Range. A series of summits in excess of 4,000 feet through The Whites that are named after American Presidents. The highest (Mount Washington) is named after the first president, the second highest the second president and so on. They are not hiked consecutively on the AT.

The Whites Huts. These are entirely different to typical AT shelters, and can be huge with multiple people staying, mostly in organized groups such as schools. They typically offer a few thru-hikers work-for-stay arrangements per night.

Trail Magic. This very well used term has specific and general uses. Specifically, it refers to food and drink that is provided (or left) on the side of the trail. It could be ex-hikers Barbequing burgers and giving them to hikers or leaving cokes in streams. More generally it refers to anything good that happens unexpectedly. The shampoo smell of a section hiker passing that gives a little moment of pleasure is Trail Magic

Virginia Blues. This describes the depression that some hikers experience in Virginia because it is the longest state and seems never ending. It illustrates the importance of celebrating milestones such as when state lines are crossed.

War of 1812. The War of 1812 was fought between Britain and the new US. Several battles were fought in Virginia.

Warren Doyle. Is an institution on the Trail. He holds the informal record for hiking the AT the most times. Eighteen times with 9 thru-hikes and 9 section hikes. He has led 10 groups on thru-hikes. He founded the Appalachian Long Distance Hikers Association, and the Appalachian Trail Institute.

Water filter. Nearly all water consumed is from streams and should be filtered. I filtered all my water as I had had giardia before and did not want to repeat the experience. I used various types until I settled on a Sawyer mini. It is important not to allow filters to freeze as they can lose their effectiveness and become unsafe.

Whalebacks. Long, smooth mounds of rock rising up from the ground like a whale breaching the sea's surface.

White Blazes. The trail is marked by a 165,000 white blazes (2x6 inches). That's one every 70 feet on average. There is no need for a map on the AT, although a Trail Book is vital.

Work-for-stay. The practice of working at the hostel instead of paying cash.

Zero Day. A day with no miles hiked. It usually is accompanied by the first laundry and shower for several days, plus food resupply. Post-zero blues is the depressed feeling hikers sometimes get after their zero day. One's pack it at its heaviest and normally contains a week's food.

3

MAP OF THE APPALACHIAN TRAIL

MAX MASON

HAPPY HIKER

MAX MASON

4

THE CAST OF CHARACTERS

The photos show some
of my fellow AT thru-hikers

Gravity, Columbus, Rabbit, Doc, Boston.

Mofo, Pilgrim and Mungo

Around the circle L-R – Mongoose, ?, Runs with Beers, McFly, ?, Happy, ?, Amish.

Walking Home, Walnut, McFly, Lean To, Chocolate.

Sam I Am, All The Way, PapaAl, PhilCo, Walnut, Red Hot.

Walnut, McFly, Old Eagle Scout, Happy, Walking Home.

5

THE HAPPY HIKER EPIC POEM

State 1 Georgia

DISTANCE - 78 MILES,
CUMULATIVE DISTANCE SO FAR - 0
PERCENTAGE COMPLETED - 0%

FRIDAY, 20 MARCH 2015

Day 1. Stover Creek Shelter. GA. 2.8m

Why fly from half a world away
And hike two thousand miles?
Why leave a job, and all you know
For many months of trials?

I want to see the seasons change
Immersed in nature's game.
At mid-life point it's not too late,
So starts my path to Maine.

Mount Springer's rain drizzled down,
The first night far from home,
The shelter's way too full for me,
I'm cold and feel alone.

Day 2. Hawk Mountain Shelter. GA. 5.4m

Hawk Mountain proved my pack's too full,
I'll throw out what I can,
Then at Long Creek I dropped to rest,
And met a special man.

He said his name was Mountain Dew,
And kind eyes lit his face.
He was a Baptist "Praise the Lord,"
Convinced of his God's grace.

He said, "Let's hike together friend,"
"And see Katahdin's Fall."
I said, "Okay…" but thought the worst –
He never preached at all.

Day 3. Gooch Mountain Shelter. GA. 7.7m

At dawn, I crawled out of my tent,
Which was so warm and dry,
The mountain frost was promising,
A chill to freeze the sky.

My friend was waiting with his Book,
And standing in the dew,
He was packed up and keen to hike,
His name I knew was true.

Horse Gap was steep, a long descent,
Up Justus made me sweat,
My clothes came off and on and off,
By dark I'm cold and wet.

Day 4. Lance Creek camp. GA. 8.5m

An early start for Preaching Rock,
My new friend loved the name.
Big Cedar's views, and Woody Lake,
All met with our acclaim.

We joined up with Tattoo and Shades,
Who spoke to Mountain Dew.
Their Trail Names were discussed at length,
They then asked, "How 'bout you?"

They say a rose by any name,
But I'll need something snappy,
To psyche me through the toughest times,
So now they call me Happy.

Day 5. Neel Gap. GA. 7.4m

Blood Mountain had a tale of woe,
And so did Slaughter Creek,
Some battles won and others lost,
I wished the hills could speak.

We found our peace at Woods Hole hut,
And learned of murder foul,
A hiker girl* eight years ago,
I hope she's peaceful now.

Earl Schaffer* hiked in forty-eight,
His soldier's soul was sore,
He needed peace and solitude,
And so, walked off his war.

Day 6. Low Gap Shelter. GA. 11.5m

Neel Gap's boot tree and outfit shop*,
A nice motel so warm,
A beer, a bed, a steamy shower,
No fear of any storm.

Tattoo and Shades, me and old Dew,
We're dry and warm today,
In just a week, friends through and through,
Katahdin's months away.

Look for the blaze*, your beacon light,
Go back if they're not seen.
I've learned to hike big hills real slow,
You'll crash if you're too keen.

Day 7. Unicoi Gap (Hiawassee). GA. 9.7m

Up, up we trekked, the Mountain Blue,
Four thousand feet on high,
We saw blue tents down in the Gap,
"Trail Magic!" was our cry.

Free food and drink, with smiles and cheer,
These folks just love the Trail,
They help us hike, that's their reward,
They serve so we prevail.

Are people good or are they not?
I know this much is true,
The Appalachian Trail is there,
To find the best in you.

HAPPY HIKER

Day 8. Hiawassee. GA. 0m

The Budget Inn, Hiawassee,
Oh, I felt a hero,
A whole day off – I'd earned my stripes,
Hiking to my zero!*

Remember I'm a stranger here,
And everything is new.
No kilometers or Celsius,
No I don't have a clue!

No time to rest, the whole day's shot,
All You Can Eat, with brew,
We launder and buy too much food,
And then our trek renews.

Day 9. Deep Gap Shelter. GA. 13.1m

All day it rained, I hiked alone,
Felt weak and had no grit,
It conquered me: post-Zero blues,
I thought, "It's time to quit".

I'd go back home, and limp a lot,
Shot knees would be my tale,
I'd blame bad luck which can't be helped,
Why I had left the Trail.

Then up ahead, Tray Mountain's track,
I'm thinking to depart,
An amputee with a metal leg,
Pours shame into my heart.

Day 10. Plumorchard Gap Shelter. GA. 8.1m

She's Bionic, she saved my soul,
We shared some repartee,
She manned me up, reframed my mind,
That gutsy amputee.

I hiked ahead, the sun came out,
The sky was cobalt blue.
We all have grit, I've found mine now,
I'm sure I can hike thru.

Caught up with Dew who loved the wild,
He'd lived and knew it all,
Red bud and beech and how birds flew,
He hiked and was in thrall.

States 2 & 3
North Carolina & Tennessee

North Carolina and Tennessee share their state line with the AT at times, and so this section shows both states as one.

DISTANCE - 309 MILES

CUMULATIVE DISTANCE SO FAR - 78 MILES

PERCENTAGE COMPLETED - 4

MONDAY, 30 MARCH 2015

Day 11. Standing Indian Shelter. NC. 12.5m

Throughout the night coyotes howled,
Come dawn, I saw one clear,
He looked through me, streaked down the hill,
Raced past and saw my fear.

So Dew and I walked out the state,
Coyotes left behind,
GA/NC, thirteen to go,
But Georgia's on my mind.

The Trail was tough, the laurel thick,
My shirt was wet with sweat,
Saw Muskrat Creek then set up camp,
Remarked on the sunset.

Day 12. Betty Creek Gap. NC. 11.3m

We stayed together up the hill,
As Dew had hurt his back.
Please hold his site at Betty Creek,
I set off down the track.

I hiked alone, looked at the views,
Saw young Tattoo and Shades.
Where is Dew now? There was no word,
I waited for decades.

At Carter Creek the journal's blank*,
And Betty Creek was clear,
The shelter's bare, an empty nook,
How could he disappear?

Day 13. Winding Stair Gap. NC. 12.2m

All night I thought, "Was I so wrong?"
At dawn "What will I do?"
Had I misheard? He was so tough!
There was no Mountain Dew.

No signal on my mobile phone,
I thought, "What would he like?"
I was alone, and on my own,
Maybe 'Hike my own hike?'*

I missed his smile, his white-haired chin,
But I've no food at all.
I head for town, leave Dew behind,
So far, my toughest call.

Day 14. Franklin. NC. 0m

I booked into a Microtel,
In Franklin for a rest.
Old Dew then called – his back was Hell,
"Go on", he said, "it's best."

I shopped and ate, with heavy heart,
A zero day alone,
I watched TV, thought of my pal,
His AT hike was blown.

The week ahead would be quite tough,
And I'd need a Sawyer*,
My filter froze. It's time to go,
Shuttle's at the foyer.

Day 15. Wayah Bald Shelter. NC. 11.0m

A long slow slog, five thousand feet,
At Swinging Lick a break.
A heavy pack, there's too much food,
At Wayah Bald, I ache.

I loved the Bald's* three-sixty views,
Horizons far away,
Sublime sunsets, but why no trees,
Grow on these hills today?

A mystery shroud, a grassy mane,
A blue infinity.
The ridges that we see afar,
Are our eternity.

Day 16. Nantahala Outdoor Center. NC. 16.5m

A windy walk along the ridge,
Wild blossoms wave and bloom,
The air was warm, and breathed to life,
The young in nature's womb.

Spring Beauty pink, and Bloodroot white,
Trout Lily leaves and jewels,
Green buds flow up from down the Gap,
Feeding life's renewals.

Long path downhill not many spills,
Nantahala's next.
Sixteen point five, my best day yet,
More miles than we expect.

Day 17. Sassafras Gap Shelter. NC. 6.7m

I partied late, too much craft beer,
First light I'm just awake,
I'm stumbling up the long, cruel trail,
And see my first black snake!

Through Grassy Gap to Sassafras,
I chanced to meet Square Hand,
We ate some smores, and then he said,
His kidney's worth ten grand!

His organ sold to cover costs,
So cash is in the bank.
Green Man was there, with friend Offie,
They thought he was a crank.

Day 18. Cody Gap. NC. 12.0m

Sweetwater Creek, Stecoah Gap,
Then Jacob's Ladder next,
The Bible says, it was a dream,
Jacob was perplexed.

The Ladder drained out all my zest,
I wondered why I'm here,
I read Zach Davis' lists aloud,
So doubts would disappear.

The deluge came, it was a dump,
The final mile's a run.
I pitched my tent, soaked to the core,
And thought, "That wasn't fun!"

Day 19. Fontana Dam. NC. 8.7m

I woke up wet, but in the sun,
And pleased to feel the breeze,
A bit of wind can help your hike,
It dries your tent with ease.

Fontana Dam seen from on high,
Means we can hike down fast,
I started well then tore my thigh,
Oh damn, I was aghast.

We booked into Fontana Lodge,
With Offie and Green Man.
They brought me food and cheered me up,
Their humour dry, dead-pan.

HAPPY HIKER

Day 20. Fontana Dam. NC. 0m

The greatest fear of mine was that,
A wound would halt my hike,
The stats weren't good, three-quarters failed,
A thought I didn't like.

I barely moved, I tried to rest,
I needed to come right,
The boys tried hard to raise my mood,
I whined and was uptight.

Green Man then spoke about his life,
Brought me to earth I'll say,
A year ago, he'd lost his spouse.
My whining went away.

Day 21. Mollies Shelter. TN. 12.3m

Fontana has a claim to fame,
A movie on the dam,
But Fugitive* was not shot here,
When Ford was on the lam.

We signed into Great Smoky Park,
Where trees and mountains reign,
Boulder jumbles, throne-shaped rocks,
My thigh in constant pain.

We liked Shuckstack, and stopped for lunch,
Fresh donuts, and swiss cheese,
We looked for bears but saw no sign,
Just ragged holes in trees.

Day 22. Derrick Knob Shelter. TN. 12.0m

From Mollies Ridge to Russell Field,
Old Offie talked all day,
My leg had healed, but then we found,
Green Man had lost his way.

We climbed up high on Thunderhead,
And waited for our friend,
Then carried on, yet yearning back,
We needed to descend.

At Derrick Knob Offie turned back,
To find his thru-hike friend,
But Green Man needed insulin:
Their trek was at its end.

Day 23. Mt. Collins Shelter. TN. 13.8m

Head in the clouds, I roamed off track,
Into a sea of cars,
It's Clingman's Dome, the tourist trap,
I felt I was on Mars.

Appalled I stared at all those souls,
And paused to sip a drink,
One stared at me – she's fat and pale,
And said out loud, "You stink!"

Back on the ridge, I called my wife
Her humor would be apt,
She said something, it was so small,
Enraged I boiled and snapped.

HAPPY HIKER

Day 24. Newfoundland Gap. TN. 4.5m

All night I seethed, then settled down.
And tried to figure why,
I'm normally such a laid-back chap,
And wouldn't hurt a fly.

These mountains need an act of will,
Not for the faint of heart,
One needs to find another gear,
Or you may as well not start.

My new-found strength comes at a cost,
My mood is on the edge,
But love should temper anything,
I'll need to make that pledge.

Day 25. Townsend. TN. 0m

I called my wife to seek a truce,
And longed to see her face,
She then flew down to Gatlinburg,
For me to share her grace.

When she arrived we hugged and laughed,
And I apologized,
She knows I am not easily riled,
And said she was surprised.

She knows the Trail needs strength of will,
To drive yourself each day,
A new persona quite intense,
For battle and the fray.

Day 26. Townsend. TN. 0m

We went for drives to see the park,
Ate well and loved to talk,
The problem was she liked to stroll,
And I refused to walk!

We planned her hikes along the Trail,
She lived in Boston then,
Her research job gave her the time,
To visit me again.

Reluctantly we had to shop,
Then homeward for a nap,
A pulled-pork lunch and trying not,
To think – Newfoundland Gap.

Day 27. Tri-corner Knob Shelter. TN. 15.6m

Newfoundland Gap was our goodbye,
I'm overwhelmed and wept,
I've never felt this way before,
With rain and tears I'm wet.

Charlie's Bunion can't be seen,
The storm it hammered down,
The trail became a river deep,
And if I slip, I'll drown.

The saddest day went on and on,
At last Tri-corner Knob,
The shelter's packed, two dozen deep,
A sullen soggy mob.

Day 28. Cosby Knob Shelter. TN. 7.5m

In pouring rain I pitched my tent,
I was alone and sad,
But in my tent, it was quite dry,
Then thought, "It's not that bad."

You won't hike thru if you're too sad,
Can't keep on spiraling down,
You need to focus on the task,
And choose to lose the frown.

Hiked past a plane wreck in the bush,
My mind's back on the job,
I'm focused now, the trail's downhill,
I'm close to Cosby Knob.

Day 29. Spanish Oak Gap. TN. 14.7m

There's nothing like a long downhill,
To make the spirits soar,
Three thousand feet, from peak to creek,
It's Spanish Oak by four.

I bought a book on flowers and trees
But don't know where to start,
The world is green, buds everywhere,
The Trail is in good heart.

Deep down I know it's why I'm here,
Like Henry James Thoreau,
To lose myself in nature's thrall,
Like he did long ago.

HAPPY HIKER

Day 30. Walnut Mountain Shelter. NC. 17.0m

No other tents – I'm fine with that,
You see I'm not alone,
The birdsong brings a rowdy dawn,
Each pair must build a home.

This mountain has a Snowbird name,
Its spring is Wildcat too,
Then Turkey Gap and Groundhog Creek,
It's nature through and through!

We've said goodbye to Smoky Park,
I didn't see a bear,
But that's OK, I'm quite content,
With birdlife in the air.

Day 31. Hot Springs. NC. 13.7m

It's very steep up Walnut hill,
I hate those damn false summits,
My inner voice then lifts me up,
Before my spirit plummets.

Next morning I was feeling good,
A downhill day ahead,
I aim to make Hot Springs, the town,
And find myself a bed.

Part through the day, I saw blue tents
Which caused a joyful grin,
Trail Magic is a welcome sight,
My spirits lift within.

Day 32. Spring Mountain Shelter. NC. 11.0m

A cheap motel, a long hot shower,
Eat at The Iron Horse.
I can relax, no need to think,
Where's my next water source.

I listened to the TV news,
The anchors did agree,
They said it was the wettest spring
Since 1870.

The ground was soaked, more trees would fall,
And hikers might be killed,
It happened just a month ago.
I felt a bone deep chill.

Day 33. Jerry Cabin Shelter. NC. 15.4m

Sometimes a shelter crowd just clicks,
Last night was just like that,
We pitch our tents and gather round,
It's laughter, flames and chat.

I met Benjali, Doc and Sticks,
Young Rabbit, then her Mom,
The girl was only sixteen years,
And blessed with such aplomb.

Those Blackstack Cliffs were fearsome high,
Just past Bearwallow Gap,
I worried then that I would fall,
A terminal mishap!

Day 34. Hogback Ridge Shelter. NC. 15.2m

I'm getting fit, my trail legs strong,
I power up the hills,
I need more food, for energy,
Which means those extra bills.

My friends at work, around the world,
Can't help but take a look,
My weekly posts and photographs,
Are teasers on Facebook.

I have no job, I'm fifty-five,
I'm learning to be free,
And grateful for the time I have,
To seek who I can be.

Day 35. Bald Mountain Shelter. TN. 10.1m

I love to sleep inside my tent,
Except when it rains hard,
But snoring in the shelters means,
You're always on your guard.

And it can't be much fun for those,
Who have a youthful bladder,
Old coots like me who have to go,
Disturb and make them madder.

It's rats that share the shelters too,
Because it's such a drag,
To nibble on a Snickers Bar,
Then rehang your food bag*.

Day 36. Uncle Johnny's Hostel. Erwin TN. 17.1m

Three thousand feet we'll drop today,
With seventeen miles to town,
Then zero on the day to come,
And hills today just down!

Bald Mountain drops to Whistling Gap,
Then past No Business Knob,
We'll bed at Uncle Johnny's place,
And see the hiker mob.

I'd met Miss Janet a week ago,
Helping her hiker brood.
Don't mention her at Johnny's place,
A Tennessean feud!

Day 37. Uncle Johnny's Hostel. Erwin. TN. 0m

The red nosed male receptionist,
Gave me some rum – I think.
He welcomed me to Johnny's place,
Clearly, they like to drink!

The party was well under way,
Though it was only three,
It carried on 'til early hours,
There was no sleep for me.

There was a fight with Trixie's son,
He probably was too young,
Her dog Gertrude was also there,
With bloodhound's drooling tongue.

Day 38. Beauty Spot Gap. TN. 12.3m

Post zero blues and heavy pack,
As usual weighed me down.
The Nolichucky River shined,
Below near Erwin town.

I trudged a thousand feet uphill,
To Curley Maple Gap,
There were wildflowers everywhere,
I saw a Dutchman's Cap.

Another thousand feet of climb,
To Beauty Spot campsite,
The crowd that camps in cars were there,
It doesn't seem quite right.

Day 39. Clyde Smith Shelter. TN. 13.9m

A thousand feet to start the day,
Up through Unaka's spruce,
Ethereal views of blueish hues,
In layers light diffuse.

I love big trees of every shape,
They fill my soul with joy,
To see and smell, and hear and touch,
My wonder unalloyed.

There's balsam spruce with birch and beech,
Pine, oak and hickories.
They are all one, a forest whole,
Not lonesome soli-trees.

Day 40. Little Hump Mountain. TN. 18.0m

Roan Mountain is six thousand feet,
Our camp was in the cloud,
I was the only older bloke,
The rest were young and loud.

Chewy, Doc and Captain Planet,
Kept us entertained,
Others smoked some pot that night,
Their laughter unrestrained.

There're two main groups of hikers here,
The younger and the old,
One's average age is twenty-two,
Then fifty-five I'm told.

Day 41. Elk River camp. NC. 14.7m

The prospect of a downhill day,
Just makes me want to sing.
A Cafe Happy at Elk Park,
Brings effortless hiking!

I called ▢my▢ café from the trail,
And thought I'd need to walk.
They said, "Oh no, the chef can drive",
Now that's the way to talk!

Roan Highlands spoke to me today,
Recalling my dear Dad.
The quartz rock and his prospecting,
When I was just a lad.

Day 42. Moreland Gap Shelter. TN. 12.3m

Elk River camp was quite sublime,
Long grass so soft and green,
I need no mattress to drift off,
The river sounds unseen.

Next day there's water everywhere,
I barely have to think,
Of filling up my Camelbak,
When I stop for a drink.

The sky was looking ominous,
I feared there'd be a gale,
I ran for Moreland's Shelter then,
But didn't expect hail!

Day 43. Pond Flats Campsite. TN. 11.3m

Me and Johnny Adventure hiked,
He loved photography,
We shared our lives as hikers do,
And our biography.

He asked to stop at Black Bear Lodge,
I said "Okay, let's,"
A pizza and a video,
'Twas, "As Good As It Gets."

We stopped that night at Pond Flats camp,
But Johnny was unwell.
The next day he said: "Carry on",
I did but felt like Hell.

Day 44. Turkeypen Gap camp. TN. 16.3m

I'm racked with guilt much of that day,
I should have shown more care,
And wondered how poor Johnny was,
It really felt unfair.

At what point do you stay or go,
When you have made a friend?
My visa was for just six months,
I might not make Trail's end.

The signs along the path were blunt,
No stopping at the lake,
The bears were bad, so hike on through,
No chance to take a break.

Day 45. Abington Gap Shelter. TN. 18.9m

By now each day has its routine,
I wake up, eat my food,
Then fill the pack, shake out the tent,
If moisture has accrued.

Each day was planned to some extent,
For water and for lunch,
Most hikers tend to walk apart,
But eating's in a bunch.

I plan to get to Abington,
A day of nineteen miles,
It's quite a haul, but nice and flat,
And hopefully no trials.

State 4
Virginia

DISTANCE - 619 MILES,
CUMULATIVE DISTANCE SO FAR - 465 MILES,
PERCENTAGE COMPLETED - 21%

MONDAY, 4 MAY 2015

Day 46. Damascus. Cabins. VA. 9.9m

Ex-servicemen are on the Trail,
Away from all the strife,
And Twister was a chopper man,
With stories of the life.

I so enjoyed my chat with him,
We really seemed to click,
I hoped to see him down the trail,
But Man, he hiked too quick!

I loved the day before the rest,
When zero's in the air,
To find a room with good TV:
Damascus hear my prayer!

Day 47. Damascus. Cabins. VA. 0m

Damascus is a hiker town,
That much is cast in stone,
And Trail Days is their May event,
A massive party thrown.

To make it I would lose a week,
I can't afford the time,
Far better to lift up mine eyes,
And from the valley climb.

The AT is Damascus' Road,
Some will find damnation,
Others God or just themselves, and
Name it their salvation.

Day 48. Lost Mountain Shelter. VA. 16.1

I left town on the Creeper Trail,
And hauled my hefty pack,
A thousand feet up Iron Mount,
Then ate my Twinkie snack.

I loved the rhododendron trees,
And wondered what's inside,
I hadn't seen a bear as yet,
They're quiet and like to hide.

At six pm a thunderstorm,
We're just two miles from camp,
The rain no longer bothers me,
I'm Happy, dry or damp.

Day 49. Thomas Knob Shelter. VA. 12.4m

We're four states down, with not much wrong,
Except Virginia Blues.*
We see more hikers bailing out,
They feel they've paid their dues.

I'm sad to see the steady stream,
Of spaces in the line.
If you can master all your thoughts,
You surely won't resign.

I hiked with Doc and Gravity,
We saw snakes intertwined,
Then Rabbit and Columbus joined,
Mount Rogers was a grind.

Day 50. Hurricane Mountain Shelter. VA. 15.4m

Now Robie1 and Hooti were,
The funsters of the Trail,
They always were so positive,
A laugh without a fail.

We met quite early in the piece,
Lost Mountain if I'm right,
We'll climb Katahdin in the fall,
And share our great delight.

The Grayson Highlands are a treat,
A landmark on the way,
The ponies are so cute, but wild,
They're free and so they stray.

Day 51. Partnership Shelter. VA. 18.8m

Near Sugar Grove and Marion,
The shelter's Partnership.
We ordered pizza. What a treat.
Then turned in for a kip.

The youngsters talked all night it seemed,
About conspiracy,
The world had just one government,
And no democracy.

The young folk slept in late again,
The oldies hit the trail.
Unlike the tortoise and the hare,
They'll pass us without fail.

Day 52. Atkins. Motel. VA. 11.1m

I'm hiking solo mostly now,
And love the end of day,
To chat to hikers that I know,
Then eat and hit the hay.

The hikers start in pairs or groups,
Each person's pace their own,
Then slowly spread out on the trail,
And spend the hours alone.

The overtaking has a theme,
It's usually on a slope,
If like a tortoise up the hill,
It's downward at a lope.

Day 53. O'Lystery Pavilion camp. VA. 12.2m

I left the motel with a box,
And looked for the Post Office,
I sent my winter clothes away,
Warm weather's now a promise.

Wearing shorts was now the norm,
And tee-shirts all you need,
My pack was lighter; so was I,
It's time to up my speed.

I see Trail Magic at a church,
These Methodists are good,
They knew our need, to feed and leave,
A hiking brotherhood.

Day 54. Davis Farm camp. VA. 18.7m

I started late, but aimed to hike,
A twenty-mile day,
Two thousand feet up Chestnut Knob,
I'm fit so it's child's play.

I hadn't planned my water well,
There's nothing on the crest,
When darkness fell, I saw a torch,
It was a girl, distressed.

She had no water or a map,
Was clueless where she was,
I gave her all I had to drink,
Then slept beneath the stars.

Day 55. Helveys Mill Shelter. VA. 18.8m

I had no water all that night,
No breakfast, nor a clean,
Then three more miles to find a creek,
I glugged and felt serene!

At Laurel Creek and Trail Boss Trail,
There was a noisy valley,
With stripes and tails and cheep, cheep, cheep,
It was a chipmunk alley!

At Helveys Mill the crowd were men,
Plus Gravity and Rabbit,
They handed out marshmallows then,
And that became a habit.

Day 56. Trent's Grocery Trailer Park. VA. 16.2m

I love Virginia, I've no blues,
Today there were two deer,
The ridge is flat, the weather's good,
Perhaps I'll see a bear...

The hikers from last night arrived,
At Trent camp's Grocery,
I feel content, this is my crowd,
A hiking coterie.

We camped within the trailer park,
It seemed benign at first,
Then in a pair of Harley's roared,
They were both drunk and cursed.

Day 57. Woods Hole Hostel. VA. 15.2m

I met my Helen on the trail,
Feeling like a hero,
We hosteled at serene Woods Hole,
Longing for a zero.

Up on the trailhead were red lights,
An ambulance it seems,
A young man with a Bowie knife,
His thigh, a cut, some screams.

Slipped on a rock, an accident.
His knife strapped to his thigh,
My hiking friends grinned at his plight,
So much for that tough guy!

Day 58. Woods Hole Hostel. VA. 0m

There is no pleasure quite as sweet:
A zero with a car,
We shuttled hikers around the town,
Spent too long in a bar.

We drove to West Virginia state,
And did the tourist thing,
We ate and slept and talked a lot;
I dreaded our parting.

I wondered why I felt this way:
A strange propensity,
To feel much more, a heightened state,
This Trail intensity.

Day 59. Rice Field Shelter. VA. 18.0m

To Perisburg I hiked with her,
And slack-packed* all the way,
We talked of ticks and Lyme Disease,
Spread DEET* without delay.

The deer tick is the curse of all,
Some friends had left the trail,
With fever, headache and stiff joints,
The bullseye* told the tale.

We said goodbye, choked back the tears,
I wished that I was stronger.
Like childhood days at boarding school,
When tears were always conquered.

Day 60 Bailey Gap Shelter. VA. 16.5m

Each day the greening ground's profuse,
With vines and blades and stems,
The old, dry mat of winter leaves,
Replaced by living gems.

Black snakes and rattlers, garters too,
But just one copperhead,
Box turtles, skinks and all those frogs,
I take care where I tread.

Before the rain a miracle,
A newt in tangerine,
A warning that, "I'm poisonous,"
A salamander teen.

Day 61. Laurel Creek Shelter. VA. 14.6m

Today it's rocks that set the scene,
My ankles taking strain,
The hiking poles make such a din,
The clicking grates my brain.

The steep ascent before our lunch,
Is steady and unmarred,
But as light dies this mountain gets
More steep and twice as hard.

The twilight brings me to my knees,
Despair is in control.
Then shame recalls, "You have two legs,"
Bionic frees my soul.

Day 62. Craig Creek camped. VA. 14.3m

My evening pall and state of mind,
My spirit battleground,
Is fertile in the dwindling day,
When hunger's to be found.

I need to rest and eat trail mix,
Three hours after lunch,
The calories are energy:
My body's counterpunch.

I pat the massive Keffer Oak*,
Into the past I delve,
Two centuries ago it saw,
The War of 1812.*

Day 63. Four Pines hostel. VA. 14.9m

Young Audie Murphy's from these parts,
A hero from the war,
He went 'To Hell and Back*,' in life,
Though barely five foot four.

His monument is on the Trail,
Before the Dragon's Tooth,
He died at only forty-five,
And that's the saddest truth.

Yes, Four Pines hostel is a mess,
You can't deny that's true,
With couches scattered round the room,
But laughter's blowing through.

Day 64. Lamberts Meadow Shelter. VA. 16.3m

McAfee Knob's the place for pics,
Most famous on the Trail,
And in this age of imagery
It is the Holy Grail.

Your family and your friends will say,
You're brave and resolute.
At first you'll think it's just a pic,
A small part of the route.

Then years will pass and things will change,
The image of the rock,
And you will find it slows right down,
The ticking of the clock.

HAPPY HIKER

Day 65. Daleville. HJ Motel. VA. 9.1m

The AT is a moving feast,
And Trail Names come so fast,
They hike too quick, too slow, or leave,
Each chat could be the last.

To find firm friends who hike your speed,
And greet you with a smile,
When you slog into camp at night,
Makes it feel worthwhile.

For months and miles, I'd shared their pace,
A trailworld we cohabit,
But it's goodbye, their school has called:
Gravity and Rabbit.

Day 66. Daleville. HJ Motel. VA. 0m

My boots are shot, it's time they went,
Do I buy boots again?
There's rocks ahead, but light is best,
Would shoes* see me to Maine?

I have a day, it is a zero,
Outfitters* here I come,
Salomon, Brooks, Sportiva, Keen,
My brain is feeling numb.

So Merrill Moab's my new shoe,
Protecting me from rocks,
The salesman has a skillful tongue,
Darn Tough* are my new socks.

Day 67. Wilson Creek Shelter. VA. 11.2m

I've armed myself with song downloads,
The Daleville wifi's great,
But then I hear the saddest news,
Of Joan Dodd's cancer fate.

It's Memorial Day, USA,
My thoughts are far away,
A good New Zealand friend has died,
Can't keep my tears at bay.

A family friend of grace and poise,
I can't believe she's gone.
My body aches, just like my heart,
Don't feel like hiking on.

Day 68. Bryant Ridge Shelter. VA. 20.8m

Blue Ridge Parkway then Blackhorse Gap,
I'm walking with Grey Goat,
We pass the Peaks of Otter view,
My thigh is sore, I note.

Bearwallow Gap delivers food,
Trail Magic tastes so sweet,
And ice-cold cokes sit in the stream,
The moment is replete.

This twenty-mile day's a first,
I'm secretly quite pleased,
The cost is pain, my thigh is stiff,
The ache is unrelieved.

Day 69. Harrison Ground Spring. Camp. VA. 13.4m

Drugstore and Whisper helped me out,
Painkillers in my hand,
"New shoes and twenty miles today?"
They said in reprimand.

Grey Goat hiked on to my regret,
My pace was just too slow,
The Guillotine*, and Thunder Hill,
Just adding to my woe.

The pills were gone, I had to stop,
The pain too much to bear,
My Appalachian dream is moot,
Oh, please God, hear my prayer.

Day 70. Glasgow. Shelter. VA. 11.4m

I shuttled into Glasgow town,
The doctor was so kind,
I said, "I'm sorry that I stink,"
She didn't seem to mind.

She said, "It's clear you need a rest,
I'd say at least a week."
I bit my tongue and hobbled out,
Pensive, sad and bleak.

The Glasgow shelter's right in town,
With bunks and lovely showers,
The library's close, and has wifi,
To while away the hours.

HAPPY HIKER

Day 71. Glasgow. Shelter. VA. 0m

The shelter's loud, I make more friends,
But meet a sad professor,
Whose son died young, but loved the Trail,
He is his son's successor.

I didn't know that fateful day,
I'd meet some lifelong mates,
Old Eagle Scout and Walnut too,
And Sam's YouTube updates.

I'm interviewed by Sam I Am,
Who's left a prison's cordon,
And like Earl Schaffer he is now,
Walking off the warden*.

Day 72. Punchbowl Mtn. Camp Buena Vista. VA. 10.9m

I figure out a way to cheat
The doctor's week of rest,
I call a shuttle driver then,
Who helps with my request.

I'll slack-pack now and lose the weight,
Go easy on the miles,
My thigh will heal, get strong again,
To face those future trials.

So Piney Taylor rescues me,
For three days I slack-pack,
Buena Vista's my home base,
I hike then shuttle back.

Day 73. Hog Camp Gap. B. Vista. VA. 17.2m

I stealth camp* in a sports field shed,
But Piney has a grouse,
He thinks I'm cheap, and I should pay,
To stay in a guest house.

Old Piney loves to tell the tale,
When Bryson* caught a ride,
In '96 he shuttled him,
And thinks he must have lied.

'When A Walk in the Woods' came out,
And Steven Katz was there,
Old Piney laughed and said, "That's wrong,"
"Bill was alone I'll swear."

Day 74. Crabtree Falls Camp. VA. 19.1m

I bid farewell to Piney's truck,
Priest Shelter's where I'll lie,
The fifteen miles is not too far,
It won't relapse my thigh.

When I get there, I'm feeling strong,
There's light enough to burn,
I set off for the Crabtree Falls,
Just four more miles I'll earn.

At nineteen miles I've pushed my luck,
And with a heavy pack,
The thigh is healed, I'm on a roll,
This Happy Hikers' Back!

Day 75. Maupin Falls Shelter. VA. 9.0m

Last night was fun with some new friends,
Hello Onesimus,
A hiker from a while ago,
Now living in a bus.

He helped the hikers that he liked,
His Biblical name 'Useful,'
He and Trixie hit it off, and,
Really seemed quite youthful.

Now Warm-and-Toasty had some depth,
The Army in the past,
She had two cars, and flip flop* hiked,
Gave rides whenever asked.

Day 76. Waynesboro. Colony House. VA. 20.9m

It poured all day, my kit was soaked,
I'd lost my new pack cover,
A dumb mistake, it wasn't tied,
I'll have to buy another.

The deluge day drew on and on,
I'm soaked in my T-shirt,
Then Trixie passed, pulled by Gertrude,
The bloodhound's eyes alert.

I'm whacked and have a zero due,
I hitch-hike to Waynesboro,
My ride's amazed I pack no heat,
"You need a gun and ammo!"

HAPPY HIKER

Day 77. Waynesboro. Hostel. VA. 0m

I'm bone deep tired and need a break,
To sleep and read my book,
I register at Stanimals,
Before I take a look.

The hostel's owned by Stanimal,
A hiker in the past,
His bunkroom is about to grow,
Before I'm even asked.

I'm press-ganged into work-for-stay*,
This wasn't what I thought,
I'm building bunks and beds all day,
My zero's all for naught!

Day 78. Blackrock. Hostel. VA. 22.7m

I'm now behind, I've fallen back,
My thigh has cost me ground,
Slackpacking's good, to make the miles,
If I'm Katahdin bound.

I now decide to slackpack hard,
To push the next five days,
So Stanimal will shuttle me,
To catch up my delays.

The Shenandoah National Park,
And grade of Skyline Drive*,
Will hasten up my hiking pace:
Let's hope my thigh survives!

HAPPY HIKER

Day 79. Powell Gap. Hostel. VA. 17.5m

At Blackrock Park, I set my pace,
A lovely sunny day,
The trail was flat, the woods were clear,
The dappled shadows play.

Then up ahead two moving shapes,
They're gamboling on the track,
Two tiny cubs with big black ears,
But then I hear a crack.

Just to my right the mother bear,
Looks up and rushes past.
Protects her young, they disappear,
My heart is pounding fast! *

Day 80. Milam Gap. Hostel. VA. 20.6m

The Shenandoah's full of life,
The summers at its height,
I see more bear, and many deer,
It's truly a delight.

Morning birdsong fills the air,
And greets the rising sun,
Then quiet for contemplation,
Resuming, when day's done.

My favorites are the woodpeckers,
To hear their knock all day,
The thrumming drum, the blur up high,
An avian ballet.

Day 81. Thornton Gap. Hostel. VA. 20.2m

I'm moving fast, it's now routine,
A twenty-mile day,
I pass Big Meadows, buy my lunch,
They really make you pay!

Then David Spring and Franklin Cliffs,
Past Hawksbill Trail and Gap,
Up Shenandoah's Stony Man,
The highest on the map.

I pass Passamaquoddy Trail,
And muse about the name,
Another native nation with
A history wreathed in flame.

Day 82. Thornton Gap. Hostel. VA. 22.1m

Pass Mountain's really just a hill,
Elkwallow's good for food,
I think about my audio books,
And knowledge that's accrued.

My listening day has a routine,
The morning's for the Trail,
It's headphones in the afternoon,
Some music or a tale.

My favorite app is Audible,
It's stories in the main,
The better ones keep me enthralled,
I hike and feel no pain.

Day 83. Manassas Gap. Hostel. VA. 12m

The hostel at Front Royal town,
Is headed up by Mike,
We drank red wine and talked for hours,
We are so much alike.

The morning brought adversaries,
PhilCo and PapaAl,
They said my snoring kept them up,
They're blunt but what the hell.

I didn't know that we would be,
Together to the end,
I got to know them really well,
And each becomes a friend.

Day 84. Bolden Hollow camp. VA. 17.1m

The Shenandoah's now behind,
I really loved that Park,
A hundred miles in just five days,
That's now my hiking mark.

My conscience pricked, I felt quite bad,
Because I had slack packed,
But knew my thigh would not have healed,
And that's a concrete fact.

My audio book's from Tennessee,
'About The Forest Unseen,'
But right in front of me today,
That Roller Coaster's* mean!

State 5
West Virginia

DISTANCE - 15 MILES
CUMULATIVE DISTANCE SO FAR - 1006 MILES
PERCENTAGE COMPLETED - 46%

FRIDAY, 12 JUNE 2015

Day 85. Blackburn AT Centre. WV. 16.2m

Eight days without a break should mean,
I'm feeling pretty tired,
But soon I'll see my son, Mungo,
So actually, I'm fired!

He's twenty years, a fine young man,
The apple of my eye,
It's been four months, he's flown from home,
I'm such a lucky guy.

Goodbye Virginia and your Blues,
The longest state is done,
Yes, Harpers Ferry's* half-way there,
And soon I'll see my son.

Day 86. Harpers Ferry. Inn. WV. 12.5m

Today I'm hiking with my boy,
I'm Happy and I'm proud,
We walk SOBO, to Blackburn Lodge,
And meet my hiking crowd.

The Rotary have made a feast,
To eat beside the trail,
We then see Mofo and Pilgrim,
And burgers we assail.

We try to buy some beers that night,
The store won't sell us booze,
"Your son is not yet twenty-one,"
"We have too much to lose."

Day 87. Harpers Ferry. Inn. WV. 0m

We strolled around this curious town
And learned of Civil War,
Eight times it's overrun, and we,
Imagine cannons roar.

We photograph the famous sign:
AT's Conservancy,
See Potomac and Shenandoah,
Merge convergently.

We're from another land and so,
Most everything is new,
I treasure every moment, but,
I'm dreading our adieu.

State 6
Maryland

DISTANCE - 43 MILES
CUMULATIVE DISTANCE SO FAR - 1021 MILES
PERCENTAGE COMPLETED 47%

MONDAY, 15 JUNE 2015

Day 88. Rocky Run Shelter. MD. 15.4m

We had the morning to ourselves,
And then the dread goodbyes,
For four long months he's back at home,
I cross my bridge of sighs.

The Bridge to Sandy Hook leads to,
The C&O Canal,
It's flat for miles, my heart is too,
Farewells just feel like Hell.

Eventually I clear my head,
And ponder, why so sad?
The Trail cuts deep, I am laid bare,
No longer iron clad.

Day 89. Ensign Cowall Shelter. MD. 15.7m

Life must go on, I meet new friends
And then an old ally,
Old Eagle Scout, plus Runs With Beers,
And Rocky Mountain High.

Old Eagle Scout he seemed to know,
Who's shared who's tent at night,
There's really quite a social scene,
At every camping site.

When hikers talk they share a lot,
The filters disappear,
Old Eagle Scout's wife is a nurse,
Like mine so we compare.

State 7.
Pennsylvania

DISTANCE - 230 MILES
CUMULATIVE DISTANCE SO FAR - 1064 MILES
PERCENTAGE COMPLETED - 49%

WEDNESDAY, 17 JUNE 2015

Day 90. Tumbling Run. PA. 18.1m

I love the Trail in Maryland,
And Raven Rock's sublime,
Reminds me of my timeless youth,
When bush bound all the time.

You hear the banter here about,
The Mason-Dixon Line,
The North and South is still a thing,
And people still align.

I'm listening to an audio book,
American history,
But what they say, and what I see,
Can be a mystery.

HAPPY HIKER

Day 91. PATC Milesburn camp. PA. 17.2m

A splendid view from Chimney Rocks,
Then raindrops start to sting,
Will it soon stop? Perhaps persist?
Who knows what nature brings?

I've learned acceptance on the Trail,
Wisdom not felt before,
You can't control the cards you're dealt,
Just change the way you score.

Now Pennsylvania's known for rocks,
You see them through the trees,
So far the trail is fairly clear,
My worry starts to ease.

Day 92. Pine Grove Furnace. PA. 12.2m

From Milesburn Road it's not that far,
Pine Grove is just twelve miles,
AT's museum and ice cream shop:
A sweeter set of trials.

The Ice Cream Challenge* is my quest,
A test of my will power,
Consumed the quart of ice-cream slow,
<u>And</u> did it in an hour!

I love museums, but missed the chance,
To learn about the Trail,
It's history's rich, it's lessons deep,
I'll come back without fail.

Day 93. Boiling Springs. PA. 19.3m

The hike today is with someone,
Who loves to tell a tale,
He is Walnut, and he becomes,
My best friend on the Trail.

He's travelled everywhere it seems,
Adventure in his youth,
While wicked humor's in his smile,
He always tells the truth.

Our dinner's in a restaurant,
With Freebird, Teach and I,
And Redhot's walking home to Maine,
With Sam his close ally.

Day 94. Darlington Shelter. PA. 14.3m

By dawn the storm has spent its force,
There's debris everywhere,
We marvel that we weren't outdoors,
With tree trunks in the air.

We're told it is Nude Hiking Day,
And wonder what we'll see?
One hiker in his underpants,
A yawn we all agree.

This land is flat, the corn thigh high,
The storm has filled the creeks,
The landscape's lame, too many crops,
I miss my mountain peaks.

Day 95. Duncannon. The Doyle. PA. 11.3m

Walnut's knees are sore today,
But he will persevere,
For sixty-one he's very strong,
But injury's his fear.

A swollen creek laps at a bridge,
And something moves below,
A six-foot snake, thick as a thigh,
Deliberate, deadly, slow.

Tonight's a landmark of the Trail,
Duncannon and The Doyle,
This grand hotel has seen it's day,
But hikers don't recoil.

Day 96. Clarks Creek camp. PA. 18.5 m

The bar is full, and spirits high,
We're glad that we have come,
But this old lady's past her prime,
I fear for her outcome.

At Peter's Mountain there's a hut,
It's huge with second floor,
We're hiking past when rain pours down,
And we race for the door.

I meet a soldier, tall and grim,
Who tells me of Iraq,
I see the trauma in his eyes,
He lugs a cammo pack.

Day 97. Swatara Gap camped. PA. 16.8m

Now Walnut has more guts than I,
If there's a chance to swim,
He leapt into Clarks Creek that night,
Went blue in every limb!

My podcast is on climate change,
And mankind's likely end,
But then the Trail gives me some hope,
By meeting three young men.

They're Goose and Spice and Cap with bags,
Picking up the litter*,
Two thousand miles of doing good,
Smiling, never bitter.

Day 98. 501 Shelter. PA/NY City. 12.4m

I'm New York bound and Helen's there,
I sponge wash near a drain,
From 501 a new journey,
A shuttle then a train.

A neon hike right through Times Square,
Strikes me as so bizarre,
Then meet my wife and her colleagues,
They treat me like a star!

The hotel room is shelter size,
We cuddle up in bed,
She sniffs and bolts upright and then,
"Please go and bath!" she said.

Day 99. NY City. 0m

We're tourists in a foreign land,
And visit all the sights.
Big Apple in the summertime:
Unlimited delights.

We visit MOMA, and Van Gough,
Good restaurants for a bite,
But something's wrong, I feel quite strange,
And can't sleep much at night.

Three months of Trail has shown to me,
How little that we need.
So do New Yorkers need their things,
Or is it merely greed?

Day 100. New York City. 0m

Now let me tell you of my mate,
My wife she's Helen Jane,
My queen, my muse, my secret strength,
My luck to share her reign.

My priceless painting in the flesh,
My center of delight,
She's kind and good, and very smart,
My starry, starry night.

She sends me trail mix every week,
The special gourmet kind,
With her support and shining love,
- I'll never fall behind.

Day 101. Eagles Nest Shelter. PA. 15.1m

I left New York with happy heart,
I'd see my wife next week,
She's hiking on the trail with me,
For us a treat unique.

I ride back to the 501,
With Trail Angel Mary,
Midday I start, and end at eight,
My body's sore and weary.

Old Eagle Scout, Mongoose and friends,
Agree there's something wrong,
New York or here, there's not much choice.
The Trail's where we belong.

Day 102. Camp Eckville Shelter. PA. 24.5m

Port Clinton barber gives coffee,
To hikers passing by,
He patronized the girls it seemed,
Though was a friendly guy.

A quiet woman came inside,
He said, "What do you do?"
"Command a naval ship at sea",
Then made herself a brew.

The barber had no more to say,
He seemed to be deflated,
Iron Lady served her country,
And was decorated.

Day 103. Blue Mtn Summit. PA. 11m

I lost Old Eagle Scout last night,
And tented in the wet,
My miles were 24.5,
It was my best day yet.

At dawn there was a gathering storm,
Hawk Mountain is opaque.
There's dread at Allentown Shelter:
A harmless black rat snake.

A swallow's nest, the parents shrill,
The chicks are swallowed slow,
The hikers watch, don't intervene,
In nature's cameo.

Day 104. Lehigh Furnace Gap. PA. 7.2m

My wife is keen, it's time to hike,
A week along the trail,
She's spent up large at REI*,
My hints to no avail.

We hike three miles, and all is well,
Then Knife Edge looms ahead,
She scrambles up, gets to the top,
"It's bloody high," she said.

Her heavy pack, the narrow ledge,
I sense a creeping doubt,
Then there's a snake, just by her foot,
I helpfully point out.

Day 105. Mechanics Garage. PA. 18 .7m

Our stealth camp site was in the woods,
Pure nature at its peak,
A Luna moth then graces us,
They live for just a week.

The Superfund site* is super hard,
So Helen gets a ride,
With Yoda I climb Lehigh Gap,
That's coming back alive.

Mechanic John is host tonight,
His garage is our house,
Old Eagle Scout and Flyaway,
Me and my gutsy spouse.

Day 106. Camp Kirkridge Shelter. PA. 17.5m

We hiked past Leroy Smith Shelter,
And then Hahn's Overlook,
We thank Seeker and Flyaway,
Who've saved a tenting nook.

The Kirkridge Shelter's overfull,
Our tent site's far away,
Why is the trail so busy now?
Of course! A holiday!

We're on a ridge above the farms,
It's just July the Third,
But fireworks explode all night,
Their thunder clearly heard.

Day 107. Delaware Water Gap. PA. 6.1m

The Church of the Mountain Hiker,
Is where we'll sleep tonight,
A garden gazebo is our home,
With two of us it's tight.

Now it's Independence Day, in
Delaware Water Gap,
More fireworks and waving flags,
They sing and cheer and clap.

We went to sleep quite early, then,
There was a noise outside,
Reacting fast I bolted out,
"Fuck off!" I loudly cried.

State 8
New Jersey

DISTANCE 72 MILES
CUMULATIVE DISTANCE SO FAR - 1294 MILES
PERCENTAGE COMPLETED - 59 %

SUNDAY, 5 JULY 2015

Day 108. Camped Blue Mtn Lakes Rd. NJ. 16.4m

Old Eagle Scout had been to town,
And brought us back some food,
He got a fright and ran away,
Oh, why was I so rude?

Next day I tried to find my friend,
But he had hiked away,
My wife had left for home, by lunch,
I'm mortified all day.

Goodbye to Pennsylvania,
I curse your bloody stones,
Hello Advil* my new best friend,
My feet bruised to the bones.

Day 109. Mashipacong Shelter. NJ. 20.5m

From Buttermilk Falls, through Culvers Gap,
I'm wincing on the rocks,
Stony Brook Trail is so well named,
I need my Advil box.

I wish I'd bought much heavier boots,
These hiking shoes are thin,
My leaden pack drives down my feet,
To bruise the bones within.

I try to find some daily good,
Before sleep in my tent,
I saw a bear, and beaver lodge,
That lessens my lament.

Day 110. Pochuck Mountain Shelter. NJ. 19.6m

McFly and I, we hiked all day,
Goodbye Mashipacong,
The bearded German loves his cars,
He's tall and young and strong.

We resupply at Unionville,
And then we hear from Click,
His food bag ripped to shreds last night,
The bear attacked so quick.

At last I see Old Eagle Scout,
I wonder what he'll say,
He's not concerned, he shrugs it off,
My guilt is washed away.

State 9
New York

DISTANCE - 95 MILES
CUMULATIVE DISTANCE SO FAR - 1366 MILES
PERCENTAGE COMPLETED - 62%

WEDNESDAY, 8 JULY 2015

Day 111. Furnace Brook. NY. 16.6m

The Pochuck Mountain crowd is fun,
With Clover, M&M,
And Iron Lady's quite unique,
She really is a gem.

I skirt the Wawayanda swamp,
Then lunch at Heaven Hill,
A thousand feet up Stairway steps:
My Nalgene* needs a fill!

I see a crystal water creek,
And meet some new trail mates,
They're Art and Lynn or 'Two Bad Dogs,'
We share so many traits.

Day 112. Harriman. NY. Tuxedo Motel. 16.6m

We hiked along for two fine days,
And really came to gel,
We camped one night at Furnace Brook,
The mozzies buzzed like Hell!

Up The Ladder, past Cascade Brook,
This landscape is sublime,
We traipsed the whalebacks* up and down,
It was the best of times.

Art and Lynn were architects,
And now they lived to hike,
They loved New Zealand and had toured
Round on a tandem bike.

Day 113. Harriman. NY. Tuxedo Motel. 0m

We both were due a zero day,
And found a nearby place,
If quaint and quirky is your style,
Tuxedo wins the race!

I did my laundry, bought supplies,
They did those things as well,
I know we'll be the best of friends,
Some things you just can tell.

In two days' time I'll see my wife,
With Margaret her good friend,
It's just one night, but we arrange,
To meet on the weekend.

Day 114. Camp Perkins Dr. NY. 15.3m

It's farewell to the Two Bad Dogs,
Who amplify what's pure,
We'll meet again, some sunny day,
Of that I am quite sure.

I'm hiking by myself again,
Reflecting on my why,
So have I seen the Spring unfold?
OH YES, my wild reply.

I stealth camp in a grassy gorge,
Beech and birch and granite,
This is my church, my holy site,
My place upon the planet.

Day 115. Dennytown Rd. Inn. NY. 19.1m

From Perkins Tower I glimpse New York,
Then down the rocky stairs,
Bear Mountain Inn, and Hessian Lake,
And past the zoo's black bears.

I hurry by Walt Whitman's bronze,
No time for the museum,
I'd love to pause and learn some more,
So much for "Carpe Diem!"

On Hudson Bridge I hear the booms,
Of West Point military,
I'm moving fast to meet my wife,
Past Graymoor Monastery.

Day 116. RPH Shelter. NY. 10.7m

At Dennytown Road I meet the girls,
We stay at Country Inn,
Margaret's been away for years,
But still we feel like kin.

We say farewell, and set off for,
The shelter RPH,
It is that trail club's AGM,*
We get to share their cake.

Now every hiker that I know,
Is grateful for their time,
The trail maintainers volunteer,
And make it safe to climb.

Day 117. Telephone Pioneers. NY. 16.8m

Helen hikes with me all day,
And boy she does me proud,
She's feeling sick but struggles on,
Her spirit is unbowed.

Stormville Mountain comes and goes,
Then Beekman Uplands Trail,
Round Nuclear Lake, and swamps galore,
My wife's heroic tale.

The day's not done, there's no flat sites,
We pitch against the slope,
All night she's up, she's very ill,
Can't heal, but only hope.

State 10
Connecticut

DISTANCE - 45 MILES
CUMULATIVE DISTANCE SO FAR - 1461 MILES
PERCENTAGE COMPLETED - 67%

WEDNESDAY, 15 JULY 2015

Day 118. Kent. B&B. CT. 21.5m

Next day she shuttled down to Kent,
And found a B&B.
I passed the ancient Dover Oak,
The Trail's most massive tree.

I hear Scott Jurek's made his mark*,
He holds the AT record,
The Baxter Park gave him a fine,
We thought that's overboard!

The AT draws us to excel,
And Doyle* has hiked the most,
I like Pharr-Davis, as perhaps,
She's Grandma Gatewood's* ghost?

Day 119. West Cornwall. House. CT. 15.9m

My Helen's back on track today,
And I need a zero,
Her colleague has a house nearby,
So, she is my hero!

The five-mile Housatonic hike,
Is nature's most sublime,
We see a thousand shades of green,
In bursting summertime.

Wild golden rod and river weeds,
In shade of leafy trees,
The rising trout inspects insects,
And birdsong fills the breeze.

Day 120. West Cornwall. House. CT. 0m

We're told the house is near the Trail,
But really it's quite far,
Distance has more relevance,
When you don't own a car!

The house is huge, with lovely grounds,
It sure was worth the ride,
I love the smell, no reeking packs,
But leave my boots outside.

We feel so grateful we are here,
As twilight cools the air,
We sip our drinks, glance at the woods,
And see a fox appear.

Day 121. Bearded Woods Hostel. CT. 16.2m

We said farewell to Marsha's house,
And set off down the track,
A decent hike to Bearded Woods,
Where we will hit the sack.

Through another Lemon Squeeze,
And Sharon Mountain Road,
We're hiking well, with energy,
In super-hiker mode.

The Housatonic's crossed once more,
Mount Prospect's up the hill,
Then Rand's View and Giant's Thumb,
And Bearded Woods hostel.

MAX MASON

State 11
Massachusetts

DISTANCE - 91 MILES
CUMULATIVE DISTANCE SO FAR - 1506 MILES
PERCENTAGE COMPLETED - 69%

SUNDAY, 19 JULY 2015

Day 122. Bearded Woods Hostel. MA. 16.9m

The hostel's name is made of bones,
They serve a tasty stew,
The owners love to hike as well,
They're Hudson and his Lu.

My Helen hikes with new friends found,
Rawley and Sassafrass,
Iron Lady shares her past,
I like her gravitas.

I love this hike, up on the ridge,
The laurel and the views,
Mount Everett and the waterfalls,
"Life's good," I softly muse.

HAPPY HIKER

Day 123. Beartown Mtn Rd. MA. 18.9m

We're shuttling up to Jug End Road,
When Hudson gets a text,
It's Lu – there's hikers acting weird,
He frowns and is perplexed.

Suddenly he sees the light,
We screech a fast U-turn,
We race back home, but it's OK.
I'm touched by his concern.

We've seen those hikers on the Trail,
They shuttle all the time,
There's something off, they're too intense,
I guess it's not a crime.

Day 124. Washington Mtn Rd. MA. 24.2m

Helen hikes half day with me,
Then shuttles to the end,
The Cookie Lady picks her up,
And finds another friend.

Today's quite flat, just two big climbs,
Although we started late,
There's Baldy Mountain then Beckett,
And Helen took my weight.

I think of Helen as I hike,
Tomorrow she goes home,
She hikes so well, I'll miss her smile,
And now I'll be alone.

Day 125. Cheshire. Catholic Church. MA 18.3m

The Cookie Lady rents her lawn,
And gives away baked goods,
In dark and drizzle the future's bleak,
When I walk out of the woods.

Old Eagle Scout, and friend Walnut,
Are waiting with my wife,
And so I see I'm not alone,
My smile comes back to life.

Two towns we walk through in a day,
And pause at both to feast,
Then hostel at the Catholic Church,
And meet the coolest priest.

Day 126. Sherman Brook Camp. MA. 16.3m

Mount Greylock looms, with monument,
The highest in the state,
A good steep climb, with hands and feet,
With restaurant food as bait.

Slumped in the sun, out of the wind,
We eat our greasy fries,
Sightseers who ascend in cars,
Regard us with surprise.

The curious ones will pause to talk,
And marvel at what we do,
Their timid partners move them on,
With eyes that fear the new.

HAPPY HIKER

State 12
Vermont

DISTANCE - 149 MILES
CUMULATIVE DISTANCE SO FAR - 1597 MILES
PERCENTAGE COMPLETED - 73%

FRIDAY, 24 JULY 2015

Day 127. Bennington. Autumn Inn. VT. 16.8m

Into Vermont, and the Long Trail,
We see sticks on the track,
Sixteen hundred miles it says,
But no food's in my pack.

We're due another zero day,
Before we can resume,
Old Eagle Scout, Walnut and I,
We book a motel room.

I shower first then walk back in,
The room before I think,
The smell's a wall, an awful thing,
"My God you people stink!"

Day 128. Bennington. Autumn Inn. VT. 0m

At home I had a public role,
And knew the press quite well,
I thought they may just like to hear,
The story I can tell.

The library had the internet,
Though it was very slow,
I crafted up a press release,
And hoped that it would go.

We had Ramunto's burgers and
Three beers that upped my mood,
But then a journo phoned me back,
And I was interviewed!*

Day 129. Kid Gore Shelter. VT. 14.4m

Some time ago I found a phone,
Just lying near the track,
The word went up and down the trail,
And Ice-fire tracked it back.

Of all the people that I met,
This man had my respect,
Legally blind, and now retired,
All help he would reject.

I asked myself when times were tough,
What would Ice-fire do?
He'd carry on no matter what,
And just keep hiking thru.

Day 130. Stratton Pond Shelter. VT. 15m

We hiked with Ice-fire down the trail,
Then slowly pulled ahead,
It must be tough, when you can't see,
The place you have to tread.

The biggest duty of the day,
When Stratton Mountain's done,
Was thanking Benton for his dream,
In nineteen twenty-one.*

MacKaye dreamed big, the naysayers scoffed:
His footpath dream would fail.
But Avery*, he built it all,
The Appalachian Trail.

Day 131. Manchester Centre. VT. 10.7m

We booked into Green Mountain Inn,
And now I have to brag,
The owner Jeff he raises high,
A big New Zealand flag!

The crew was there: Old Eagle Scout,
And Walking Home, McFly,
Yoda she of Lehigh Gap, and,
Walnut my ally.

I'll share the loft with you, McFly,"
Said Yoda with a grin,
He blushed, but really had no choice:
There's no room at the Inn.

Day 132. Little Rock Pond Shelter. VT. 19.5m

We wander through Green Mountain State,
And see ski slopes with grass,
We meet a hiking family,
That no one can surpass.

There's ten in all, and seven hike,
The youngest he is nine,
The oldest kid is seventeen,
Then Mom and Dad in line.

They're Simple Man and wife Chocolate,
The girl is Lollipop,
The boys are Turbo, Tigger, Dash,
Mud Magnet's the full stop.

Day 133. Whistle Stop Restaurant campground. VT. 12.6m

The Family starts each day the same,
And Simple Man starts first,
They usually hike the trail in pairs,
By evening they're dispersed.

The Dad's a doctor with strong faith,
They never hike on Sunday,
They're structured and quite focused too,
It's 'back to work' on Monday.

You hear their laughter though the woods,
They're bright and brave and bold,
A lesson when the Trail's feels tough –
Mud Magnet's nine years old!

HAPPY HIKER

Day 134. Rutland. 12 Tribes Hostel. VT. 17.4m

Today we tackle Killington Peak,
I've been here once before,
Last Christmas with my family,
And there was snow galore.

Now it's T-shirts, shorts, green grass,
It's like a world away,
We're on the Peak, the tourists stare,
Its sure not Groundhog Day.

We book into 12 Tribes Hostel,
Unsure what to expect,
Some say a cult, but all I see,
The shirts are mostly checked.

Day 135. Rutland. 12 Tribes Hostel. VT. 0m

12 Tribes were different yes that's true,
But they were very kind,
They took us in, they gave us food,
And didn't charge a dime.

Jesus freaks without the drugs,
They prayed and sang at meals,
They shared their wealth, and didn't preach,
It's action that reveals.

By now my feet were very sore,
They've grown an extra size,
I take Advil four times a day,
Some say that that's unwise.

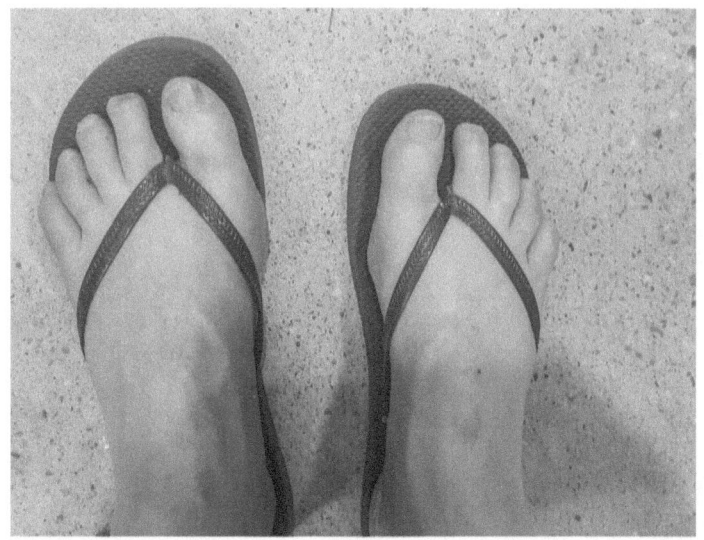

Day 136. Camp. Wintturi. VT. 17.3m

Quimby Mountain is a strain,
I have no energy,
I don't know why; I've eaten well,
So why my lethargy?

I call my wife to say goodbye,
She's flying as she planned,
Her research in the States is done,
It's back to New Zealand.

"It's just six weeks," I say to her,
"And then I'll be at home,"
"But you are home to me," she says,
"And I'll be there alone."

Day 137. White River, W. Hartford, VT. 19.0m

The daily faces on the trail,
We come to recognize,
For those who quit are sadly gone,
And we have new allies.

Our bubble* is the older guys,
Walnut and PapaAl,
Old Eagle Scout and All The Way,
And Red Hot who's Sam's pal.

Old soldiers Philco, Walking Home,
They once were GI Joe,
Hooti hiked with Robi1,
Then Pilgrim and Mofo.

State 13
New Hampshire

DISTANCE - 161 MILES
CUMULATIVE DISTANCE SO FAR - 1746 MILES,
PERCENTAGE COMPLETED - 80%

TUESDAY, 4 AUGUST 2015

Day 138. Days Inn Hanover, NH. 9.9m

Last night we camped at Randy's house,
White River flows on past,
Walnut and Sam jump from the bridge,
Like kids they have a blast.

Some like to hike alone it seems,
There's Lean To and McFly,
Our speed's the same, except for those,
Late starters flying by.

Hanover is a generous town,
Free food at each snack bar,
It was Bill Bryson's home, but shame,
He never hiked this far.

Day 139. Moose Mtn Shelter. NH. 10.9m

Last night we slept five in a room,
Then hiked the Trail through town,
The only Ivy League it sees,
Is Dartmouth* and its gowns.

I hiked with Walnut all that day,
And learned more 'bout his life,
Two great kids, and two black labs,
And Marty his fine wife.

We've hiked a dozen states so far,
And feel close to the end,
But we all know New Hampshire has,
Great mountains to ascend.

Day 140. Hexacuba Shelter. NH. 17.7m

Each day it's good to have something,
To carry in your mind,
The Ice-cream Man about half-way,
Helps put the miles behind.

The pink flamingo points the way,
We ate and then reclined,
Why give ice-creams to passers-by?
I think just to be kind.

Seeing the kindness on the trail,
Restores my faith and zest,
Smart's Mountain looms, I take it on,
And pause upon the crest.

Day 141. Welcome Hikers. Glencliff, NH. 14.8m

Mount Cube's a thousand feet uphill,
And then we reach the crown,
I'm the fast one up the hills,
And Walnut's quicker down.

I pick my way down the incline,
And Walnut flies right by,
Then trips and faceplants on a rock,
His nose is bent awry.

His hiking poles are in his pack,
Perhaps he'll use them now,
But not a chance, he mops the blood,
And hikes on anyhow.

Day 142. Camp Lost River Rd. NH. 9.3m

I met a friend before the hike,
Joe Fubel is his name,
He's hiked the AT once before,
And never was the same.

He started running marathons,
Then ultras were his game,
And he became a family man,
With loving well his aim.

In Boston he shook down* my pack,
And helped me save some weight,
He's come to Moosilaukee Mount,
To hike the Granite State.

Day 143. Franconia Notch. NH. 16.3m

The Whites are just as brutal as,
The stories would suggest,
Each day the trail is steeper and,
We climb a higher crest.

Kinsman Mountain's double tough,
Two peaks at north and south,
A steep descent with slippery rocks,
My heart was in my mouth.

The darkness hid I-93,
When we got down the hill.
Walking Home's wife picked us up,
So kind, and what goodwill.

Day 144. Econolodge. Lincoln, NH. 0m

At last a zero, our feet can rest,
We're all a little tense,
Then Walnut snaps at Eagle Scout,
For just a small offense.

They patch it up and all is well,
We eat a gargantuan lunch,
The other diners glance at us,
This fractious, hairy bunch.

The rule of thumb – we're four-fifths done,
But only half the pain,
The Whites are pretty tough so far,
And then a month in Maine.

Day 145. Econolodge. Lincoln, NH. 0m.

The weather Gods hurl down the rain,
We'll rest another day,
It's dangerous to hike in this,
Though it's a day's delay.

I think about my hiker friends,
So high up in the hills,
Wet granite worn from countless boots,
Means injuries from spills.

We sleep away the deluge day,
Or catchup on FaceBook,
A friendly tribe of followers,
Sneak in those weekly looks.

Day 146. Garfield Ridge. NH. 10.3m

Three thousand feet with heavy packs,
Up to Franconia Ridge,
No views today, just driving rain,
And colder than a fridge.

We teeter on the knife edge track,
Then slow down to a crawl,
Steep drops both sides, a monstrous wind,
I pray nobody falls.

Ascending to Mount Lafayette,
And then the slow descent,
Slippery, dangerous, nerves on edge,
My spirit's nearly spent.

HAPPY HIKER

Day 147. Ethan Pond campsite. NH. 14.5m

When we slog in, the shelter's full,
Of hikers and their grins,
The shelter journal's in Sam's hands,
And tells of murderous sins.

The story's dated yesterday,
By Dirty Rotten Liar.
Called 'Murder in the Great Rainstorm,'
There's chuckles round the fire.

Next morning we can't find the trail,
It's now a waterfall,
So inch by inch down through the spray,
On hands and knees we crawl.

Day 148. Nauman campsite. NH. 9.3m

Today's the challenge of The Whites
The Presidential Range,*
The sky is blue, and I just hope,
The weather doesn't change.

Three thousand feet plus Webster cliffs,
Then our crew pause for lunch,
PapaAl keeps us amused,
Oh man, I love this bunch!

The AMC* are at Mizpah Hut,
They say to join us please,
They're celebrating fifty years,
But we just steal their cheese.

Day 149. Madison Spring Hut. NH. 11.8m

Mount Washington* is viewed with dread,
With weather so capricious,
A morning storm's forecast and so,
The signs are not auspicious.

Lakes of the Clouds is our Plan B,
But we don't see the storm,
Then on the summit a cycle race,
An unexpected swarm!

A donut then to Madison Spring,
Cross boulder fields, which hurt,
At the Hut it's work-for-stay* but,
Man that manager's curt.

Day 150. Pinkham Notch hostel. NH. 7.8m

Last night we scrubbed the dirty pots,
Slept in the dining hall,
My morning's job to wipe the beds,
A candy wrapper haul!

From Madison peak to Osgood site,
Then down to Peabody,
The trail is boulders, stones and rocks,
My feet are pain embodied.

At Pinkham Notch the shuttle comes,
And takes us to 12 Tribes,
They see we're tired, and give us food,
I like their low-key vibes.

HAPPY HIKER

Day 151. Camp Carter Dome. 6.6m

It's been five days, a zero's due,
We started late again,
A brutal climb to Wildcat Ridge,
My feet in constant pain.

"You don't conquer the mountain,"
Sir Edmund Hillary stressed,
"You conquer yourself," and he should know,
As first up Everest.

I leaned my pack against a birch,
And ate a Snickers Bar,
A turkey family gobbled by,
Katahdin's not that far.

Day 152. White Mtns Hostel. NH. 14.5m

Before I go to sleep each night,
I read my AT Guide,*
By AWOL Miller who hiked through,
It's always by my side.

The elevation of the trail,
Is profiled very well,
Then every detail you could need,
To daily doubts expel.

The secret is to play mind games,
And look for positives.
I like downhills and zero days,
Those are my narratives.

Day 153. White Mtns Hostel. NH. 0m

We've nearly hiked two thousand miles,
And soon will be in Maine,
What have I learned? It's hard to tell,
I guess, to live with pain.

I'm learning to control my thoughts,
By watching from above
When I feel bad and hate the hike,
I look for things to love.

I've just one fear – an injury,
Could bring this to an end,
Apart from that, I'm focused on,
That mountain to ascend.

Day 154. Gentian Pond Shelter. NH. 11.9m

White Mountains Hostel's in Gorham,
The hanging packs sure stink,
The hostel's great, we laugh a lot,
We'll be okay I think.

I make the most of zero days,
Although there's not much time,
To read is such a luxury,
By dark it is bedtime.

I was born in Zimbabwe,
My family's good and kind,
I miss my Mom, and sisters too,
They'll soon have peace of mind.

Day 155. Full Goose Shelter. NH. 9.6m

Before dawn broke at Gentian Pond,
I filled my CamelBak,
The surface of the pond's like glass,
Then there's a vee-like track.

Like scissors cutting silk at night,
Beneath a moonlit sky,
The vee heads straight at me and then,
Looks deep into my eye.

I've seen the lodges from the trail,
But never seen one live,
I hold my breath, hear footsteps come,
She thwacks her tail and dives.

MAX MASON

State 14
Maine

DISTANCE - 282 MILES
CUMULATIVE DISTANCE SO FAR - 1907 MILES,
PERCENTAGE COMPLETED - 87%

FRIDAY, 21 AUGUST 2015

Day 156. Grafton Notch. Pine Ellis. ME. 9.7m

Today's momentous in two ways,
The first is Maine's state line,
The AT's longest mile is next,
I hope it is benign.

A jumble of great rocks crunched in,
A deep forbidding gorge,
Formed by volcanos, steam and time,
The Devil's fiery forge.

A pile of moose bones welcomes us,
And Walnut checks his watch,
It takes two hours, it's tough but fun,
We've done Mahoosuc Notch!

Day 157. East B Hill Rd. Pine Ellis. ME. 9.3m

Yesterday's the last state line,
It's time for some reflection,
For me five months of wilderness
Affirmed my wild connection.

When Red Hot crossed the line he wept,
For all roads lead to Rome,
The magnet of his state pulled hard,
So too for Walking Home.

Our Youtube man is Sam I Am,
We're all his biggest fan,
From prison guard to media star,
He is a special man.

Day 158. South Arm Rd. Pine Ellis. 10.1m. ME

Our speed in Maine has slowed right down,
The miles per day is half,
There's cliffs and climbing every hour,
Not for the faint of heart.

The effort's worth the price to me,
The bush is dense and wild,
The wonder of the wilderness,
Makes me a timeless child.

His family cabin is close by,
And Redhot cooks a meal,
Sitting in a chair is rare,
A short respite to heal.

Day 159. ME 17 Oquossoc. Pine Ellis. ME. 12.4m

By now my wife can feel my strain,
And wants to fill my cup,
From New Zealand across the world,
So Helen sets it up.

All our family and all our friends,
Made a Facebook post,
It was a photo of themselves,
And said what meant the most.

My Mom and sisters and their friends,
Make posts in Zimbabwe,
Our friends in in Europe and at home,
All motivated me.

Day 160. Farmhouse Inn. Rangeley. ME. 14m

It's farewell to Pine Ellis house,
They hosted us so well,
We're bound for Rangley's Farmhouse Inn,
Four nights it's our motel.

I love the whalebacks * here in Maine,
With berries small and sweet,
Walnut likes to push on through,
But I slow down to eat.

We pass by famous Moxie Pond,
The jokes fly thick and fast,
The Mainers all defend their drink,
Whose flavor's unsurpassed!*

**Day 161. Perham Stream. Farmhouse Inn.
Rangeley. ME. 15.3m**

The cliff face after Eddy Pond,
Has ladders as an aid,
On Saddleback you see those views,
Diffuse to blues then fade.

The granite ridge gives promises,
But each is a false summit,
By end of day your hope's at bay,
And then it starts to plummet.

As hopes fade with the dimming light,
When tired and least at ease,
You'll see those phantom shelters then,
Illusions through the trees.

Day 162. Caribou Valley Rd. Farmhouse Inn. Rangeley. ME. 8.6m

Lone Mountain's bush is deep and dense,
It hides Spaulding Lean To,
The shelters names have changed in Maine,
We shrug and hike on through.

The Farmhouse Inn is what we need,
Good shuttles and good food,
The kitchen means we cook our own,
Grilled veggies boost my mood.

Now there's a dish all Kiwi's know,
There's nothing like lamb roast,
I feed my friends a mighty feast,
But I don't like to boast...

Day 163. ME 27, Stratton. Farmhouse Inn. Rangeley. ME. 8.3m

Death on the Trail is fairly rare,
Far less than in the city,
Some accidents, some heart attacks,
Today I'm filled with pity.

There's a notice near the trail,
It's Geraldine Largay,*
She disappeared two years ago,
What happened on that day?

Like life we're in the wilderness,
Though some just see romance,
These mountains take no prisoners,
You get no second chance.

Day 164. East Flagstaff Rd (near Little Bigelow Lean-to). ME. 16.7m

The Bigelow's have some repute,
As daunting as they look,
Three thousand feet to Avery Peak,
And up from Stratton Brook.

We marvel at the sky-blue views,
Above the Flagstaff Lake,
Then end the trek before we planned,
But my feet really ache.

The shuttle's going to be an hour,
I see an icy stream,
My feet slide in, the pain abates,
The pleasure's like a dream.

Day 165. West Carry Pond Lean-to. ME. 8.7m

The journey from trailhead to town,
When due a resupply,
Can be by shuttle at a cost,
Or hitchhike on the sly.

In some states along the Trail,
They say it is a crime,
But we got rides so frequently,
We did it all the time.

Most of my friends were pretty raw,
But Happy was the master,
In my youth I hitched a lot,
Which means I'll get there faster.

Day 166. Stirling Inn. Caratunk. ME. 14m

From Carrying Pond Portage Trail,
Of Benedict Arnold* fame,
Past picturesque Pierce Pond stream,
The Kennebec is our aim.

This river is real wide and so,
Us hikers must canoe,
There is a white blaze painted on,
So purists* will keep true.

Walnut has hiked the Trail complete,
My friend's straight as a die,
Each day he starts the place he left,
His head he can hold high.

Day 167. Bald Mountain Brook Lean-to. ME. 14.7m

My mornings still remain the same,
Absorbing natures gifts,
Then after lunch it's ear pods,
That help me climb those cliffs.

My favorite app is Audible,
Non-fiction in the past,
But Maine's so tough and I'm so sore,
That tales keep me steadfast.

I need my stories like a drug,
Today it's Game of Thrones,
It's yarns transport me to new worlds,
That don't have aching bones.

Day 168. Horseshoe Canyon Lean-to. ME. 13m

Putt Putt and Tumbles hike our pace,
We see them every day,
And there is something bugging me,
I'm baffled and can't say.

Then I realize what's my beef,
It's what's in AWOL's Guide,
Last night I saw the trail profile,
It looked an easy ride.

Those expectations raised my hopes,
Then they were dashed alas,
But now I see so I reframe,
I know, "This too shall pass."

**Day 169. Lakeshore House Hostel. Monson. ME.
9.0m**

We ford the Piscataquis stream,
Then hike round Hebron Lake,
The Hundred Mile Wilderness,
Is next, but first, our break.

We're sad this is our last zero,
The moment is quite poignant,
But Monson calls and sadness won't,
Inhibit the enjoyment!

Its Friday night and Pete's Place hums,
Live music not downloads,
My band request is from my youth,
Our home of country roads.

Day 170. Lakeshore House Hostel. Monson. ME. 0m

The feeling of the hikers now,
Is glad and bittersweet,
Katahdin's now in striking range,
And all have aching feet.

Yes we're tired in every way,
And dream of no more rocks,
But we don't want this hike to end,
A crazy paradox.

We arrange for resupply,
And eat a lobster roll,
I pray we'll see no injuries,
That add more to the toll.

Day 171. Camped near Long Pond Stream Lean-to. ME. 15.3m

I see young Wallet at Long Pond,
It's been months since the start,
He's found a girlfriend on the Trail,
And boy, she stole his heart.

I puzzle on the human mind,
His girlfriend bailed in Maine,
She'd had enough, has left the Trail,
It was a crying shame.

Through Big and Little Wilson Streams,
The ford's a single rope,
Our boots come off, the torrent's deep,
We cling to lifeline's hope.

Day 172. West Branch Pleasant River. ME. 15m

*Alone I walked by mossy rock,
And it absorbed me whole,
It showed to me the Universe
And sounded in my soul.

It spoke of the connective force,
That makes the many, one,
How I was rock and it was man,
All things warmed by the sun.

I now saw clear what I had glimpsed,
Compassion, Kindness, Love,
Those forces that bind all of man,
To climb those peaks above.

HAPPY HIKER

Day 173. East Branch Lean-to. ME. 16.4m

At Pleasant River yesterday,
Our last hike resupply,
A shuttle brought food for my friends,
Just five days from goodbye.

Gulf Hagas Mountain and White Cap,
Then there's the perfect view,
Mount Katahdin seen at last,
So why am I subdued?

Our friends Hootie and Robie1,
Camped near Walnut and I,
My wet clothes chafe, the river's cold,
I soak my feet and sigh.

Day 174. Potaywadjo Spring Lean-to. ME. 19.5m

For months my friend and I have hiked,
Out from our camp each day,
But this morning Walnut's left,
Why has he gone astray?

I worry if I've done something,
To make him feel irate,
Then down the Trail he appears,
So sorry for the wait.

It's just a simple trail mistake,
But made me feel offended,
The fault is mine – too quick to judge,
It's time this Trail was ended.

Day 175. Rainbow Stream Lean-to. ME. 18.2m

Yesterday was tough terrain,
Not-to-mention those big miles,
My friends are worn, their bodies ache,
It's hard to draw their smiles.

We coin a phrase, "Thru-hikers groan,"
When lifting up your pack,
The bones compress, the tendon's shriek,
And pain shoots through your back.

Last night it rained, so tents are wet,
Then on throughout the day,
But there's that smell, in Maine's wet woods,
A natural bouquet.

Day 176. Abol Bridge campsite. ME. 15m

I thru-hiked for the wilderness,
And now I've had my fill,
But it's those hikers that I've met,
Who're inspirational.

Trail Pilgrim is a giant to me,
He leads the Warrior Hike,
An ex-Army Chaplain man,
He's highly authorlike*.

He started with a dozen vets,
To try walk off the war,
He helped them cope and find their feet,
Their souls, and peace and more.

Day 177. Katahdin Stream. AT Hostel in Millinocket. ME. 9.9m

From Abol Bridge past streams and falls,
I'm savoring each moment,
My rocks, my trees, my birds, my leaves,
Is there no postponement?

Walnut's sad but not too bad,
His Georgia's near to hand,
I'll never hike this Trail again,
I'm from a far-off land.

We pass a car park in the sun,
And Walnut needs a snack,
He yogi's* up a tourist pair,
My friend sure has the knack!

Day 178. Mount Katahdin. Hostel in Millinocket. ME. 5.2m

The final push is just five miles,
Although up five thousand feet,
A mighty pile of granite rocks,
Our journey is complete.

We kiss Katahdin's famous sign,
And pose for photographs,
So many of our friends are here,
There's tears and awkward laughs.

Our slow descent is in a daze,
Thoughts, feelings, cannot speak...
The realization is ablaze
I reached Katahdin's peak!

The following day. 178 + 1. Boston. MA

The long drive down I95,*
In hours what took us months,
Marty drives and Walnut talks,
My answers mostly grunts.

I dread this part, the last goodbye,
I like this man so much,
A true comrade, a mighty man,
I hope we keep in touch.

In Boston I'm with Sam I Am,
Who hosts me for the night,
I love his home – the best man cave,
The outdoors, his delight.

MAX MASON

6

EPILOGUE

MAX MASON

HAPPY HIKER

My last night in the USA,
Is where it all began.
With Joe and Molly and their kids,
A close and loving clan.

And so my journey ended then,
Or maybe just begun,
Another man, a stronger man
Emerges to the sun.

What did I learn, what have I gained?
I know this much is true.
Your mind is stronger than you think,
That's why you can hike thru.

Doubts and pain and obstacles
Have all been overcome,
I found a strength, deep in us all,
My new time has begun.

Empowered now, and confident,
I'll take on other tests,
At home, at work, in living well,
Every day will be my best.

I see connections with all things,
It was there all the time,
It just took hardship and some pain,
For me to unveil mine.

It's true, you may not always win
But you will never fail.
Stride from your comfort zone and find
YOUR Appalachian Trail.

MAX MASON

7

This poem is an expansion of the three-stanza poem on Day 172

AN INFINITE MOMENT ON PLEASANT RIVER

That morning I was by myself,
And musing on my soul.
I'm walking by a mossy rock,
And it absorbs me whole.

This rock is living, it's not dead,
The trees and water one.
The minerals and the meteors,
All things warmed by the sun.

MAX MASON

All time and motion ceased to be,
The truth was manifest.
All things connected by a force,
With which they are all blessed.

The greatest thing was certainty,
I didn't doubt the truth.
I think I glimpsed this long ago,
Before I lost my youth.

This unity is not just for,
The natural universe.
It's you and me and all mankind,
We're really not diverse.

And all religions seek the same,
Compassion is the core.
Our paths are different we agree,
But love binds even more.

This timeless moment slowly fades,
I feel less independence.
I'm part of something bigger now,
The Trail bestowed transcendence.

GLOSSARY

Day 5 – Meredith Hope Emerson (24) was murdered near Blood Mountain in 2008. Since 1974 there have been 11 murders on the Appalachian Trail.

Day 5 – Earl Schaffer was the first person to thru-hike the AT. He saw action in the Pacific in WW2 and said he hiked the whole distance of the AT in 1948 to "walk off the war".

Day 6 – Neel Gap has an outfitter shop and a tree with hundreds of old boots hanging from it.

Day 6 – The trail is marked by a 165,000 white blazes (2x6 inches). That's one every 70 feet on average. There is no need for a map on the AT, although a Trail Book is vital (see Day 152 for description of Trail Books).

Day 8 – A zero is a day with no miles hiked.

Day 12 – Every shelter has a shelter journal. Hikers write their names and times of arrival and departure plus notes on weather conditions or to friends. Their function is safety related as they record where the last place of a missing hiker may be. Shelter journals can be very entertaining.

Day 13 – Hike your own hike is a common saying on the AT. It means you have permission to make decisions for your own benefit without fear of criticism. For example, leaving behind a slower friend if they are nursing an injury.

Day 14 – A Sawyer is a brand of water filter. It's important not to allow them to freeze. I filtered all my water as I had had giardia before and did not want to repeat the experience.

Day 15 – Balds refer to the grassy tops of otherwise thickly wooded hills. It is a mystery why some balds exist, where similar nearby hills are completely covered with forest. Balds allow hikers to experience rare views.

Day 21 – Fontana Dam was reputed to be the location for the Harrison Ford movie, 'Fugitive'. Actually, it was nearby Cheoah Dam.

Day 35 – Shelter rats thrive when hikers don't place all their food and packaging in sealed food bags hung from bear cables outside. Rats are attracted to discarded food wrappers at night. A rat ate through a zip on my pack to get at a Snickers bar I had forgotten in the hip belt pocket.

Day 49 – Virgina Blues describes the depression that some hikers experience in Virginia because it is the longest state and seems never ending. It illustrates the importance of milestones such as when state lines are crossed.

Day 59 – DEET is a popular insect repellent to control deer ticks. One survey found 9% of hikers contracted Lyme disease. Some get treated and can return to hiking. If not treated it can cause a range of long-lasting heath issues.

Day 62 – The largest oak tree on the AT in the southern states is about 300 years old.

Day 62 – The War of 1812 was fought between Britain and the new US. Several battles were fought in Virginia.

Day 63 – Audie Murphy was one of the most decorated soldiers in WW2. To Hell and Back was a movie he starred in, playing himself, when he returned from the war.

Day 66 – Outfitters are outdoors recreation retailers.

Day 66 – Darn Tough are a well-known brand of hiking sock.

Day 69 – The Guillotine is a rock passage with a suspended rock above hikers who have to squeeze through.

Day 71 – Sam I Am was a recently resigned career prison warden who thru-hiked to walk off the negativity of prisons. He video interviewed hundreds of hikers (see Youtube). He also wrote an excellent book, 'Sole Searching on the Appalachian Trail.'

Day 59 – Slack-packing is the practice of hiking with an almost empty pack. All the heavy items are transported by other means to the next shelter. It's frowned on by purists who believe you should carry your full pack all the way.

Day 73 – Stealth camping is sleeping in a non-designated or illegal area.

Day 73 – Bill Bryson wrote a best-selling book 'A Walk in the Woods: Rediscovering America on the Appalachian Trail,' in 1998. Many thru-hikers resent the fact he made money from the book but only hiked 870 miles. His hiking companion in the book was Steven Katz, who some say did not exist.

Day 75 – Most thru-hikers start at the south terminus of the Trail and hike north in one sequence. They are called Northbounders or NOBOs. About 20% start at Mt Katahdin and hike south and are known as SOBOs. A few flip flop hike which refers to the practice of hiking a mix of non-sequential sections of the Trail, but who complete the full distance in one calendar year. Warm-and-Toasty had two cars, and would drive one north, park it at the trailhead, and hike south to the second car. She would drive that to a trailhead about a day's hike beyond the first car, and repeat the process.

Day 77 – Work-for-stay is the practice of working at the hostel instead of paying cash.

Day 78 – Skyline Drive is the road that runs through or near the Shenandoah National Park. It was built during the Great Depression to create jobs at about the same time as the AT.

Day 79 – There is a video of my mother bear and cubs incident on:

https://www.nzherald.co.nz/bay-of-plenty-times/video/black-bear-spotted-on-the-appalachian-trail/Y2ZV3V75JYWJL4DUCZY76W666M/

Day 84 – The Roller Coaster is a 12.5 mile section with 3500 vertical feet of steep up and down hills, mostly 300-400 foot ascents and descents.

Day 85 – Harpers Ferry, WV is the psychological mid-point of the Trail. The Appalachian Conservancy (which administers the AT) is located there. It changed hands eight times in the Civil War and was heavily damaged.

Day 92 – The Ice Cream Challenge is a Trail tradition. The intention is to eat a quart (1 litre) as quickly as possible.

Day 98 – Goose, Spice and Cap were sponsored by Granite Gear and successfully packed out 1,090 pounds of trail trash. They would empty their bags at nearby towns recording the weight disposed of.

Day 104 – REI – Recreational Equipment, Inc., is a very popular American retail and outdoor recreation chain of stores.

Day 105 – Superfund provides the Environmental Protection Agency (EPA) funding to restore degraded sites.

Day 105 – For almost a century a zinc factory polluted Lehigh Gap with chemicals that killed vegetation and other life. Its environmental restoration was funded by Superfund.

Day 107 – A nero means nearly zero – just a short hike.

Day 108 – Advil is a painkiller. It's also branded as Ibuprofen which is known as 'Vitamin I,' as so many thru-hikers consume it.

Day 111 – Nalgene is a popular water bottle brand.

Day 112 – Whalebacks are long, smooth mounds of rock rising up from the ground like a whale breaching the sea's surface.

Day 116 – New York-North Jersey Chapter is the second largest of the 12 regional chapters of the Appalachian Mountain Club (AMC).

Day 118 – Scott Jurek beat Jennifer Pharr-Davis' Fastest Known Time by 3h13m to set a new record of 46d 8h 7m. He received a fine from Baxter State Park rangers for, amongst other things, littering when celebratory champagne touched the ground. The controversy raged up and down the Trail for months.

Day 118 – Warren Doyle holds the informal record for hiking the AT the most times. Eighteen times with 9 thru-hikes and 9 section hikes. He has led 10 groups on thru-hikes. He founded the Appalachian Long Distance Hikers Association, and the Appalachian Trail Institute.

Day 118 – Grandma Gatewood was the first woman to thru-hike the AT, in 1955, at the age of 67. She also was the first person to hike it three times. The last time was in 1963 at 75 years old.

Day 128 – My interview with the Bay of Plenty Times. They also did a feature article when I returned to New Zealand. See both below.

https://www.nzherald.co.nz/bay-of-plenty-times/news/trailblazer-nears-end-of-epic-hike/Y2FMDQEEQUUV3P2MZD3FLMVAPM/

https://www.nzherald.co.nz/bay-of-plenty-times/news/on-the-record-max-mason/RSGLEXWNKHTF77FGJUY3IDQHZM/

Day 130 – Benton MacKaye envisioned the AT in 1921 on Stratton Mountain. He was the dreamer.

Day 130 – Myron Avery was the practical doer who was most responsible for driving the completion of the AT. He was a long-time chairman of the Appalachian Trail Conference, and he both clashed and collaborated with Benton MacKaye, and others.

Day 137 – A bubble is the hiking group that roughly moves at the same speed over long distances. You may not see some people for a few days then they reappear.

Day 139 – Dartmouth College is one of eight Ivy League universities.

Day 142 – A pack shake down occurs when an experienced hiker goes through everything in a novice hiker's pack and advises what to retain or discard. It's invaluable!

Day 148 – The Presidential Range is a series of summits in excess of 4,000 feet through The Whites that are named after American Presidents. The highest (Mount Washington) is named after the first president, the second highest the second president and so on.

Day 148 – AMC (Appalachian Mountain Club).

Day 149 – Mount Washington is the highest peak in the Northeastern United States at 6,288 ft. Changeable weather and poor planning have created its reputation for a dangerous hike. Nearly 150 people have died on the mountain since 1849.

Day 149 – The Whites huts can be huge with multiple people staying in organized groups, particularly schools. They typically offer a few thru-hikers work-for-stay arrangements per night.

Day 152 – The AT Guide by AWOL Miller may be the most popular guidebook. The Appalachian Conservancy also publishes one, and various apps are also popular. They provide a wealth of information such as distance between shelters and other features, all water sources, elevation, maps of towns along the way, contact details for hostels and shuttle drivers, and a myriad of other useful information.

Day 160 – Moxie is a carbonated drink invented by a Mainer in the 1800's. It was marketed as a health drink and features Gentian as an ingredient.

Day 166 – Purists (or white blazers) are those hikers who insist on hiking every inch of the Trail, with a full pack. They will walk past every single AT white blaze. For example, blue blazes are used to mark other trails leading to shelters, views etc. Most shelters have two paths leading to and from the AT. Typically, these blue blazed trails leading to a shelter, exit the white blazed trail at an angle in the direction of the shelter. Then there is a corresponding blue blazed trail from the shelter to the Trail, joining it further up from where the exit point was. Purists like Walnut, in the morning always walked back to the point they left the Trail the previous evening and resumed their hike from there. Many purists, with the exception of Walnut, had an air of determined superiority about them. A vocabulary has arisen around the color of blazes:

- Yellow blazing – skipping portions of the Trail by hitchhiking ahead or getting a ride. This is severely frowned on by most hikers.

- Aqua blazing – missing portions of the trail by traveling by canoe or kayak. Because there is white blaze in the Kennebec river canoe, and it's compulsory, it's not considered aqua blazing.

- Green blazing – smoking pot on the AT which many young people did.

- Brown blazing – refers to hiking with an upset stomach, with frequent need to visit the bush.

- Pink blazing – seeking sex or romance on the Trail

- Bar blazing – frequenting trail towns pubs as much as possible.

Day 172 – This day I had something of a mystical experience. The daily poem summarizes it. The longer version is found in Chapter Seven.

Day 178+1 – The I-95 is the Interstate motorway running down the east coast linking most of the 14 states we walked through.

ABOUT THE AUTHOR

Max 'Happy' Mason had no endurance related successes before his Appalachian Trail thru-hike. The experience transformed him and let loose a string of firsts. He started running marathons, successfully stood for public office, became chairman of Habitat for Humanity/Doing Good Foundation, completed another ultradistance adventure by cycling across Australia (1888 miles) through the desert, wrote an epic poem and published a book.

Married to Helen and proud father of Mungo, Max was born in Zimbabwe. He served in the military, gained a B. Soc. Sc in Psychology in South Africa and M. Sc Entrepreneurial Studies in Scotland. He is a New Zealand citizen who currently lives in Australia. Max believes a positive attitude, a sense of humor and not taking oneself too seriously will solve most of life's problems.

Contact Max at *www.maxmasonauthor.com*
or *Max@mmhmason.com*

www.ingramcontent.com/pod-product-compliance
Lightning Source LLC
Chambersburg PA
CBHW021359290426
44108CB00010B/311